Ghosts of Asheville

HISTORY AND HAUNTING
OF ASHEVILLE, NORTH CAROLINA

TRACY L. ADKINS

Copyright © 2023 Tracy L. Adkins

All rights reserved.

ISBN 13: 979-8-9886845-0-3

First Printing, 2023 by Amethyst Hawk Publishing

Cover photo courtesy of Billy Sanders/Reynolds Mansion.

Interior photos by the author unless noted otherwise.

Also by Tracy L. Adkins:

Ghosts of Athens: History and Haunting of Athens, Georgia

Ghosts of Athens and Beyond: History and Haunting of North Georgia

For my Sis, Stacey,
who is the best listener in the world
and makes my life better
by being in it.

CONTENTS

Omni Grove Park Inn	1
Asheville Masonic Temple	29
Reynolds Mansion	47
Battery Park Hotel	77
West Asheville	93
The Smith-McDowell House	131
The Miles Building	147
Stonehaven: The Bynum House	153
Helen's Bridge and Zealandia	163

Acknowledgments

I extend my sincerest thanks to all those who shared their stories, knowledge, and enthusiasm that helped me compile the copious information required for this project, including the following: Ron Lambe, Lonnie Darr, Billy Sanders, Sandy Hatchwell, Rick Fletcher, Lindsay H., Tonya and Jamie, Elle, Lisa, Christina Bynum Chivalier, and my dear friend Rives Yost.

I am extremely grateful to these past and present employees of the Grove Park Inn: Miss M., Bob Barnard, Captain Bob, Beck Horne, Dusty Pappas, Joanne, Elvira Sanchez, Klara Hines, and Mary. Also, I am extremely thankful for all of my anonymous contributors who generously were willing to share their stories with me.

A humongous thank you goes out to people who have gone above and beyond in their support of my writing and books and continually assist in so many ways, including my steadfast Betwaddlers: Micah Hudson, Karen Watkins, Randy Coleman, and Bill Cody; my intrepid Beta readers: Anne Adkins, Stacey Mayes, Michael Whitlock, Sharyn Studstill, and Linda Hebb. Finally, a huge shout-out to Rachel Watkins, Janet Geddis, and the entire crew at Avid Bookshop in Athens, Georgia for their continued support.

Introduction

If you are reading this, you must have at least an inkling of interest in the unexplained. I, myself, have long been a fan of ghost stories and many times have been delighted to find a new and tantalizing book of spooky tales. I love reading about strange things that people experience but cannot explain. Some witness activity that seems to defy the laws of physics. Some hear voices of persons long passed. Some are not even sure what they experienced. I love all of these stories.

It was the love of these stories that compelled me to write my first book, *Ghosts of Athens: History and Haunting of Athens, Georgia*, which was published in 2016. Writing *Ghosts of Athens* was a wonderful experience. I was thrilled to meet and interview people who were eager to share their stories of paranormal experiences. I was fascinated by the history I uncovered when researching the historical locations. The process was fun and heartwarming from start to finish. These are also the reasons I was excited to repeat the experience by writing *Ghosts of Athens and Beyond: History and Haunting of North Georgia*, which was published in the fall of 2022.

When you are a writer of "ghost books," you always have your antenna up for new, unearthly tales and sometimes people seek you out to share theirs. I had heard of some ghost stories about Asheville before I was a local, but it was only after moving to Asheville in 2014 that I really came to appreciate the variety of haunted locales it contained. I couldn't wait to start doing research and setting up interviews and digging in to seek out the creepiest stories. Nearly ten years after beginning what turned out to be a long and winding road on the publishing journey for this collection, I am so happy to finally be able to share with you the spooky end result: *Ghosts of Asheville: History and Haunting of Asheville, North Carolina*.

The town of Asheville had its beginnings in the 1700s as a small settlement near the eastern banks of the French Broad River at a crossing of time-worn paths traveled by Cherokee traders. The North Carolina General Assembly officially formed Buncombe County in 1792 and Asheville was incorporated as the county seat in 1797. By 1827, an increase in population and travelers passing through necessitated building the Buncombe Turnpike for easier exploration. During the 1800s and on, right through to the present day, the Asheville area has seen tremendous growth, in no small part due to tourists who visit, fall in love, and decide to stay. Asheville's magnetism is not limited to enthralling its living population. Based on these stories that I have collected, it seems to trap the non-corporeal, as well.

Whether you are a true believer, a skeptic, or somewhere in-between, I am glad you have joined me on this adventure to tell the stories of the *Ghosts of Asheville*.

Tracy L. Adkins

SOME LOCATIONS MENTIONED IN THIS BOOK ARE PRIVATE.
PLEASE BE RESPECTFUL OF ALL LOCATIONS
AND OF CURRENT OCCUPANTS.

Omni Grove Park Inn

On a farm in Whiteville, Tennessee, Edwin Wiley Grove was born into poverty on December 27th in the year 1850. Grove moved to Paris, Tennessee at age 24 and worked as a clerk in a pharmacy on the courthouse square. After rising to become a partner, he eventually bought out the pharmacy, which he renamed Grove's Pharmacy.

During his time as a pharmacist, Grove saw firsthand the ravaging effects of malaria on the South. It was widely known that quinine could prevent malaria and suppress symptoms such as chills and fever, as well as destroy the malarial parasite. But, because of the bitter taste, quinine was known as "the cure that kills you." Grove sought to create a better tasting quinine treatment that would be more suitable for patients and customers.

He formed the Paris Medicine Company in 1886 and, after experimenting for several years, he developed and patented Grove's Tasteless Chill Tonic. His tonic was a liquid quinine suspension that dulled the quinine taste using iron, sugar, and lemon flavoring.

"I had a little drug business in Paris, Tennessee, just barely making a living, when I got up a real invention: tasteless quinine," Grove explained. "As a poor man, and a poor boy, I conceived the idea that whoever could produce a tasteless chill tonic, his fortune was made."

Grove's prediction was right. As soon as it became available, Grove's Tasteless Chill Tonic was hugely popular. Some claimed that by 1890, more bottles of his tonic were sold than bottles of Coca-Cola. Grove became a self-made millionaire by the time he had reached his forties.

Sales increased further when the British Army required Grove's Tasteless Chill Tonic to be issued to all troops stationed in the mosquito-infested tropics. To better handle production and distribution on a larger scale, Grove relocated the company to St. Louis in 1889.

By 1900, the Paris Medicine Company maintained offices all over the world and was the world's single-largest consumer of quinine. Grove eventually sold 1.5 million bottles of tonic after 20 years on the market.

Despite his success, Grove's life was not perfect. During his time in St. Louis, he developed health problems from bronchitis and chronic hiccups. His doctors recommended recuperation time at a summer home in Asheville, North Carolina. Soon, he established the Tasteless Quinine Company in Asheville.

Between travels to Asheville, Grove met fellow pharmaceutical entrepreneur Fred Seely in Detroit. Frederick Loring Seely was born in 1871 and began working in the pharmaceutical industry as an office assistant when he was just 13 years old.

Soon after meeting Grove, Seely left Detroit in June of 1898 to work for Grove at the Paris Medicine Company. Rumor has it that within 24 hours of meeting Grove's daughter, Evelyn, she and Seely were betrothed. They were wed in October of 1898.

Joined as family, Grove and Seely also paired up for real estate investments. Grove began purchasing properties in North Asheville with an eye toward residential development. Grove knew that with the opening of George Vanderbilt's Biltmore House, in addition to the local railroad expansion, publicity and access made Asheville a prime location for investment. By 1907, Grove owned 1,000 acres of land.

Grove and Seely discussed the idea of constructing a luxury resort. Asheville had become a popular destination, both for tourism and for travelers seeking relief from tuberculosis symptoms. However, Grove was adamantly opposed to plans to build a national tuberculosis sanitarium and threatened to stop plans for the hotel if Asheville was promoted for tuberculosis recovery. In fact, Grove purchased a number of sanitariums in the Asheville area to get rid of them and promote tourism over health resorts. In 1909, Grove purchased 408 acres that included the location that would become the Grove Park Inn.

Seeing the Old Faithful Inn in Yellowstone National Park influenced Mr. Grove's concept for his own inn. Grove's Yellowstone impressions and Seely's appreciation for the Roycroft Inn of the Roycroft Artisan

Community of New York were combined to inspire the design of their grand hotel. In 1911, Grove approved Seely's vision for the hotel and tasked him to oversee its construction. Seely promised the hotel would open its doors within one year.

On July 9, 1912 Grove's wife, Gertrude, lifted the first shovel of dirt during the ground breaking ceremony. Working ten-hour shifts six days a week, 400 men used mules, wagons, and ropes to haul granite boulders weighing thousands of pounds from Sunset Mountain to the site of the hotel. Italian stonemasons coaxed each stone into place. Workmen were instructed that every visible stone should reveal its most time-worn face.

Keeping his promise, Seely had the Grove Park Inn ready to open on July 1, 1913. Noted orator William Jennings Bryan, the Secretary of State, delivered the keynote speech at the opening. To 400 assembled VIPs at the banquet, he declared that the hotel '...was built for the ages.'"

Originally called the Big Room, the Great Hall is 120 feet long and 80 feet wide. It was, and is, the hub of social activity at the inn. Adorned with twelve copper chandeliers, the Hall is flanked by its two famous fireplaces. Each fireplace is 36 feet wide and capable of burning logs up to 12 feet long between andirons weighing 500 pounds each that were specially designed for the huge hearths. The boulders that make up the fireplaces are native granite and weigh three to five tons each. Both massive stone chimney shafts conceal a remarkable secret--a working elevator inside each one. This design was intended to reduce the noise of the elevator machinery for guests.

In fact, because Grove intended for the inn to be a refuge from unnecessary noise or distraction. In the early years, guests were discouraged from bringing small children, slamming doors, or throwing their shoes on the floor. They were even asked not to run water past 10:00 p.m.! If a discussion in the Great Hall grew too animated, the speakers were handed a small card urging them to "Quiet Down."

Decor in the Great Hall is the epitome of the Arts and Crafts style, many pieces being handcrafted by the Roycroft artisans, including an eight-foot-tall grandfather clock now valued at one million dollars. A Mission-design pool table was installed in the recreation room of the inn during 1913. Its rosewood cushion rails were chosen for their ability to withstand a lit cigar. After being moved to various locations through the hotel over the years and being sold to an employee during the 1960s, the pool table returned to the hotel in 2007 with all original racks and balls intact and is on display to this day.

Notable guests to the Grove Park Inn include Harry Houdini, Will Rogers, Helen Keller, Thomas Edison, Eleanor Roosevelt, Henry Ford, and ten U.S. Presidents. Author F. Scott Fitzgerald spent time at the inn during extended summer visits in 1935 and 1936. Booking rooms 441 and 443, Fitzgerald came to relax, to write, and hoped to resuscitate his flagging career. Staying at the inn also kept him close to wife Zelda who had been institutionalized at the nearby Highland Hospital.

After World War II, the inn was long past its heyday and falling into disrepair. The exorbitant cost to tear it down was the only thing that kept the inn standing. Then, in 1955, Dallas businessman Charles Sammons acquired the property and had the vision to restore it. In 1973, the Grove Park Inn was named to the National Register of Historic Places.

Remodeling during the 1950s and 1990s restored and expanded the Grove Park Inn, including the creation of several restaurants and a sumptuous $50 million spa. In July of 2013, Omni Hotels and Resorts acquired the Grove Park Inn and currently maintains it.

Edwin Grove died on January 27, 1927 at the Battery Park Hotel in downtown Asheville, North Carolina, but he was buried in the family plot at Paris City Cemetery in Tennessee. During his life, he succeeded at so many various business ventures, his death certificate listed his occupation simply as a "Capitalist."

When you visit the Grove Park Inn now, the Vanderbilt Atrium lobby houses a display of Grove's early medicines, including Grove's Tasteless Chill Tonic. Another notable feature of the historic Grove Park Inn is the Palm Court atrium, one of the first atrium-style hotel lobbies in the country. Beneath the atrium's massive skylight, you can see the restored original stencil work on the balcony walls, uncovered from beneath dozens of layers of paint. Long ago, when the stencils were new, a young woman fell to her death in that atrium. It was the end of a life, but just the beginning of decades of speculation about the circumstances surrounding her fall, who she was, and why she seems trapped within the walls of the inn for all time.

Often, employees hired to work at the Omni Grove Park Inn are soon told the story about the hotel's most famous ghost, the Pink Lady. The mythology of the Pink Lady began about 100 years ago. According to legend, around 1920, a woman was on the premises of the Grove Park Inn for reasons unknown.

"We have heard speculation that she was here not as a registered guest, a guest of a guest," one employee told me. "We've heard she was here as a friend of Mr. Grove, or possibly Fred Seely. The theory is that she was staying with one of them, but it was all kept very hush-hush because both those men were married to other women. That may be why the Pink Lady was not listed on the register of guests."

The story continues that the young woman was wearing a flowing pink dress when she fell, jumped, or was pushed over the railing on the fifth floor outside Room 545. She fell two stories, from the fifth floor to the third, landing below on the floor of the Palm Court atrium, where she died. According to one account, "She was rolled into a carpet and removed from the property. These things were stated in a manager's log. She never signed in; there is no death certificate and no burial plot."

One reason that the circumstances of her death remain mysterious could possibly be that, if she were a "guest" of Grove or Seely, they could have easily kept the story from being published since both men were influential and cozy with the local newspaper owners. But, even if these powerful men did use their influence to keep the story out of the news, wouldn't the young lady's family be looking for her? This question leads some to speculate that she was actually a prostitute, someone that might not be reported as missing. Perhaps this is why a few even posit that the Pink Lady is the ghost of Zelda Fitzgerald. Because there is no record, everyone seems to have their own theory about who she was and how she died. The only thing that is certain is that no one living knows the truth for sure. Only the Pink Lady herself knows the true story, and, if she ever really existed at all, she has taken the story of the circumstances of her tragic death to her grave.

Despite many questions, time and time again, guests and employees of the inn have claimed to see and interact with her for 100 years. Fortunately, these incidents are usually not aggressive or frightening. In fact, just the opposite. One guest claimed that the Pink Lady appeared and embraced them. Another suggested that when the Pink Lady appeared and startled her, the ghost tried to comfort her by holding her hand. Often, she is reported to interact gently, and even protectively, with children.

Elaine's Dueling Piano Bar is a club in the lower part of the main inn. A manager there reported seeing the Pink Lady several times over the years. "She's like a real dense smoke--a pinkish pastel that just flows. It's a real gentle spirit, whatever it is."

Beck Horne is an elevator operator at the Omni Grove Park Inn. When guests stay for several days, he gets to know them by chatting while he ferries them up and down on the elevator during their stay. "When they're here for a weekend, you get to know them a little bit," Beck said. More than one guest has shared with him stories of spooky happenings that occur during their stay.

"A young couple was staying here about ten years ago," Beck told me. "They brought their little boy with them. He was no more than four years old. The mother got on the elevator one morning by herself and she just looked at me and said, 'You'll never believe what my little boy did last night! He's never done this before!' Apparently, in the middle of the night he was sitting up on the edge of his bed, waving and saying, 'Bye bye! Bye bye!'"

That woke up the mother. "She swears she saw a pink shimmering light moving out of the room," Beck said. "I asked the mother if she knew we had a resident ghost. She said, 'No.' To me, that provides evidence or confirmation that this is real. A little kid is not gonna know. They haven't been indoctrinated, so to speak, about this."

Many employees say she is attracted to children who stay at the hotel. A college professor from Florida was visiting the hotel with her two-year old son. For two days in a row after his nap, the boy asked his mother, "Who was the nice lady?" and "Where did the nice lady go?" Of course, no one had been in the room.

One employee, Miss M., worked at Grove Park Inn for several years as a Concierge, but began her employment there by working in Reception. I asked her if she knew about ghosts at the inn before she began working there in 1999.

"Oh yeah," Miss M. confirmed. "There were probably five of us working in Reception and we always talked about the ghosts. One friend that worked in Reception told a story to me and my co-workers. One day about noon, people were checking out and a couple comes up to Reception. They were a normal, young couple with kids. They happened to stay in Room 545, the Pink Lady room.

"When people check out, we normally asked, 'Did you have a good stay? Did you enjoy yourself?' This man said, 'Yes, it was great. It was nice having a long break from the kids and we got to enjoy ourselves.' Then, the wife interrupted, 'But, we did not appreciate you sending someone to babysit when we did not ask for you to hire them.' The wife did not want to pay for an unrequested babysitting expense."

Miss M.'s friend found this strange because, normally, a guest would talk to the concierge to request a babysitter and then the concierge would assign a babysitter who would go to the assigned room. "But she didn't do that."

Perplexed, Miss M.'s friend pulled up the bill for the couple. "She told them, 'I don't think that anybody was assigned because in the bill, it should show babysitting. There is no babysitter on your bill.'"

Undeterred, the woman explained that an elegantly dressed woman in long skirts had arrived. After they went out, the woman played with the children awhile and then put them to bed. When the mischievous young boy wouldn't go to sleep and got out of bed again, she tucked him back in. The kids were asleep when the parents returned later that evening, but reported on their activities the next morning.

"My manager questioned the account of the kids," Miss M. conceded, "but, we all knew it was the Pink Lady because this had happened before. There's reports that the Pink Lady pays special attention to kids staying in that room. She likes to go there and put kids to bed. She shows herself to the kids a lot more than to adults."

Miss M. is not shocked by the likelihood of a ghost in residence in Room 545 at the inn. She has had a number of spooky experiences since her childhood. "This is a natural occurrence that happens. You cannot prove it, but these are not theories. They are things that people experience and then say, 'Well, this could be.' It's not just the spookiness or anything. Those people might be inclined towards thinking, 'Okay, there is a bigger thing out here.'"

A former front desk supervisor related a tale of one person who had an experience with the Pink Lady without having any idea there was something strange going on. He was on duty one night when a hotel guest came down to the front desk with a complaint. He said that he was not happy that the 'housekeeper' went through his room without knocking or announcing. When the guest mentioned that the 'housekeeper' had been wearing a pink dress, he bought the man a drink at the bar in the Great Hall and told him the story of the Pink Lady.

Bob Barnard is a bellman at the Omni Grove Park Inn. "I'm new here," he told me. "I've only lived here about six months. I'm retired and working here fills up my retirement. I did a lot of research by reading everything I could get a hold of about the inn. That way, when people ask me questions, I can answer them."

So far, Bob enjoys his work at the inn. "I like working here. This is a fun place. I actually get paid to do something I enjoy. You meet so many diverse people here."

As with most new employees at the inn, the veteran staff shared the story of the Pink Lady with Bob. He told me the story as he understands it.

"The Pink Lady stayed in 545. She was here to meet her lover, who was a married man. He sent her a message and he broke it off with her completely. My theory is that she didn't fall to her death, but she committed suicide. If you go up and look on the fifth floor, it's pretty hard to just fall off of that railing. It's pretty high."

I asked Bob if he thinks that it is possible she was pushed over the railing.

"I don't think so," he said. "Of the stories that have been told, the one that sticks with me the most is about a couple that wrote a letter and thanked the hotel for this lady watching her kids for three days. They described the babysitter as a woman dressed in a pink gown. The staff told her there was no lady who babysat that dressed like that."

I was very interested to hear that in the short time that Bob had been employed at the Grove Park, he had heard the babysitting story, just as Miss M. had heard it long ago.

The Pink Lady and her gown have been seen by employees, as well. Awhile back, the inn's accounting office held a New Year's Eve party. At 4:00 a.m., two employees in the office reported a sighting: "We heard someone come in the back door. We looked up and she went by real fast--a woman dressed in party clothes. We thought it was a guest, so we got up to help her. Then, she was gone."

Beck told me another story about the Pink Lady's room. "There was a woman staying here a couple months ago. She actually stayed in Room 545. She knew all about the Pink Lady and she wasn't bothered at all. Habits are habits, and she told me she always sets her glasses on the table next to her bed before she goes to sleep, just like this." Beck set down his own glasses with the arms open. "In the morning she woke up and the arms were folded closed." He folded up the glasses. "She wasn't bothered by it, she just thought it was unusual."

"You can be your own judge," he says. "I think she's quite real."

Another Grove Park Inn employee named Bob has worked at the inn for 35 years. He started as a busboy clearing tables in a restaurant called the Plantation Room.

"I worked for the Sammons family," Bob said. "Mr. And Mrs. Sammons, they just loved this place. You know, he gave the hotel to his wife for her birthday. Pretty neat birthday present! But, when he passed away, then the hotel was hers. She was a business lady and the Grove Park Inn was her special jewel that she loved."

I asked Bob if he was told any ghost stories when he came to work at the inn.

"I heard about the Pink Lady in Room 545," he said. "You don't know whether she was pushed, jumped off, fell off, or what. However it happened, it was bad that she plunged to her death."

Bob told me that, regardless of the history or rumors, guests stay in the Pink Lady's room all the time.

"545 is a regular room. Guests check in and stay in that room, to this day. They used to set that room up special for Halloween. Now, they don't really promote it as 'the haunted room'. But I've talked to several guests that have stayed in Room 545. They said they felt like someone was touching their feet every night in their sleep.

"When people hear about ghosts, they automatically think of evil things. But the Pink Lady was a nice ghost. She always made her appearances in good ways. She's kinda like Casper. The friendly ghost."

I asked Bob if he had ever had a paranormal experience himself at the hotel.

"I have worked third shift multiple times through the years, but I've never had any experiences myself. I've seen things like a picture someone took in the lobby where smoke formed like a person. And, people have talked to me about their experiences. I've heard some really good stories about the Country Club. If you go in late at night when there's nobody in there, sometimes you'll hear dishes in the kitchen rattling. I heard a story one time about one of the golf pros. This golf pro closed the golf shop one night, locked it up, and left. The following morning, he was the same one to reopen it, so, as far as he knew, nobody else had been in there overnight. But he found these little pewter statues of golf men in a circle around a candle. The candle was not lit, but that was so eerie for him. He felt like he should just get out of there."

Dusty Pappas has been an elevator operator at the Omni Grove Park Inn for about five years. She calls herself "the Elevatress." Dusty did not have to wait long after starting the job before she met the Pink Lady. After being on the job only two weeks, she was taking a woman to the sixth floor. "It was the perfect time for her to mess with me." Dusty said wryly. "Let's mess with the new girl and the woman who had too much to drink."

"The elevator is three-sided and has safety gates. When the gates are opened, even a tiny bit, that stops the elevator." Dusty explained. "And the gate is not easy to move. Do you want to try to open it?" Dusty asked me as we rode up through the chimney.

I tried it and verified that it did not move easily.

"As I took the lady to the sixth floor, the gate opened all by itself, all the way across.

"When we got to the sixth floor, the woman asked me, 'You are going to report that, right?' I said, 'Yes, that has never happened to me before.'

"All of a sudden, I felt all the hair standing up on me and I felt extremely uncomfortable. I dropped her on the sixth floor. Then, on the way back down, something was blowing on my neck. Well, I couldn't get out of the elevator fast enough. I've had paranormal experiences in the past, but I'm really cornered in this elevator. I found my boss and told him I wasn't sure if I wanted to do this job or not. He told me, 'It's probably the Pink Lady.'

"A lot of times, I will get buzzed from the fifth floor, but when I go, there isn't anybody there. We have people who are drunk and want to go to the fifth floor because of the Pink Lady. They'll be really obnoxious and say stuff, but I always defend her."

Dusty has her own theories about the history of the Pink Lady.

"I think she was probably pregnant. That's why she loves children. I think she was murdered and I think it was Grove Junior who did it," she says. "He was a horrible person. He was known to be abusive and hire ladies of the night. I think he did it or he hired someone to do it. People with money can make someone disappear, even nowadays. I think she had her neck broken up here and was thrown over the railing to make it look like she jumped, so it looked like suicide. But karma got him. Syphilis is not a great way to die."

I told her I had heard that the Pink Lady was known to frequently tickle people's feet when they stay in "her" room.

"Yes, she does that.," Dusty confirmed. "She makes noises. The TV will come on sometimes and just be a pink screen. She moves things around, gets a big kick out of that. Sometimes she appears as a pink mist, but children see her as a whole person. Even though she's seen throughout the whole resort, we have some guests who have a tradition to come back every year and reserve the Room 545. They'll bring her flowers to let her know that she is loved. The last I heard that she was seen, it was down in the basement."

I asked Dusty if she felt her presence often.

"Yeah. A lot." She answered. "And, I liked it. I used to talk to her all the time."

Although the story of the Pink Lady is centered on Room 545, she is not confined to the area of the atrium. The strange occurrences are not limited to the area near Room 545. She is seen all over the hotel.

"I'm sure there's other spirits here, besides her," Dusty says. "I've seen shadow figures upstairs, mostly on the sixth floor. But, there's different parts of this hotel that I feel very uncomfortable with. People feel cold spots where it is really cold.

"In 2016, a friend of mine was down visiting from New Hampshire. We were in a hallway looking at pictures when I heard somebody call my name. I didn't recognize the voice and it was very strange the way they said my name. I went running back to the elevator thinking somebody was going to take off with it. Then, my friend also heard my name being called."

Later, Dusty found out that, on the same night at about the same time, 8:30 at night, two people working in the Blue Ridge restaurant had a weird experience. That kitchen was being used to prepare food for in-room dining, but the restaurant was closed and empty. Nevertheless, the two workers heard the piano in the restaurant playing all by itself.

"It freaked them out." Dusty says.

The Chief of Police for Kitty Hawk, North Carolina got a surprise when he stayed in a room in the historic part of the inn. He swears that, while he sat on the bed making a phone call, someone, or something, sat down next to him.

The President of the National Federation of Press Women stayed at the inn and had a number of experiences in her guest room in the historic building, including not one, but two incidents of having her toes tickled in the middle of the night!

One couple staying on the fourth floor in 2017 reported this experience:

> "It was the middle of the night and my husband and I were just about to fall asleep, tired from our trip to Asheville. All of a sudden, I heard a sound coming from the bathroom. It sounded like my tube of lipstick rolling off of the bathroom counter, and as I heard it hit the tile floor, I thought to myself I would just pick it up in the morning. The next morning, I headed into the bathroom, but didn't see my lipstick anywhere on the floor. I reached into my cosmetics bag and there it was--my favorite shade of pink, undisturbed."

Sometimes a guest reports that they will close the window before leaving their room, but return to find it open again. "It doesn't happen very often, but it does happen," says Beck.

In the main inn, in the basement level, there is an area now primarily used for employees. "There's offices and a cafeteria," Beck told me. He related a story that another employee told to him about an experience that she had down in that area. "She was walking and she heard some footsteps," Beck explained. "As she turned around, she saw what looked like kind of a hazy figure. She said it looked like a man wearing black striped pants. I thought maybe that was somebody who worked here a long time ago. A bellman, or something like that."

I asked Beck if that happened to her recently. "That would have been within the last 12 months," he confirmed.

Another employee verifies that the basement is very creepy. "Supposedly, there's a man that walks around down there. He is tall and thin and disappears into walls."

I'll have to take their word for it. During my time at the inn, I chose, perhaps wisely, not to examine the basement for myself.

One Grove Park Inn employee, Joanne, had grown up believing in ghosts, but never met one in person. "I always believed in ghosts," Joanne told me. "Previously, I've had experiences of feelings. My grandparents had an 1810 farmhouse in New Hampshire. I spent a lot of time there and lived there off and on. You could always just feel something. I would be doing homework in the parlor, which was a small room they used on special occasions, like weddings and funerals. Sometimes, when I studied there, I'd have a feeling somebody was sitting in a chair across from me and watching me. It was so strong that I had to run out."

Joanne said she worked at the inn quite a while before she experienced anything strange there. "I was here probably two or three years and I hadn't seen a thing," she told me. "I was so jealous of other employees who told stories about their experiences." One afternoon, it was finally Joanne's turn.

"I was in the women's restroom in the main inn," she explained. "This is the part of the hotel that is from 1913, when it was originally built. There are two toilet stalls and one dressing room stall. When you walk in, the door is a push door that slams shut like an old camp door. You know, like kids camping bathrooms. Everything is just so loud in there and banging all the time."

Joanne explained that when you are at the sink, you can't see the bathroom entry door. "When you walk in, there's tall lockers blocking about five feet up. The lockers block you from seeing the sink or the toilet. You just hear somebody coming in. I was standing in front of the sink washing my hands. There's a great big mirror in front of you that lets you see if somebody is behind you. I was washing my hands when I heard someone just BAM through the door. I'd never heard anybody who was so loud, like they were in a big hurry or mad or something. So, I looked up in the mirror. I was going to say hello to whoever came in, as you do. In the mirror, all I saw behind me was this dark gray wisp. It was the size of a big curtain and flew behind me at a diagonal. It was a dark, sharp, gray shadow that went fully behind me, fast like this (she snaps her fingers). It happened so fast. Then, they went into the dressing room stall and that door slammed shut, loud. I thought to myself, 'Wow, that person was in a hurry!' As I was finishing up, I wondered, 'How could someone move behind me so fast that I could only see the shadow of them?'"

When Joanne finished washing up, she realized it was eerily quiet. "I thought, 'Gee, it's quiet in here. Is that person still here?' All these things go through your mind. I looked underneath the doors on the stalls and there was nobody there. I jumped up excited and had goosebumps because I saw my first ghost!"

Joanne has worked at the inn for five years and had this experience two years ago. "I keep hoping they will show themself to me again," she said. She mentions that several other employees in her department have had ghostly experiences. "It's like a special rite of passage here, when you finally see your ghost."

The more time she spends at the inn, the more likely Joanne will get her wish. "There's many ghosts here," she assures me. "It's not just one Pink Lady."

Beck told another story about a young family that stayed at the inn.

"It was a mom, dad, and three children who were maybe eight years old," he began. "It turns out they were triplets! Two girls and a boy. I got to know these folks. One day, the father got on the elevator by himself. He said to me, 'I gotta show you this video!' He told me that one afternoon, his wife was sitting on the bed facing the counter where the TV is. She was holding her phone and checking her email, or something. She looked up and she saw a little piece of paper on the counter moving. Something about the size of gum wrapper. Nothing big. She watched it and she decided to film it with her phone. Within a few seconds, the piece of paper just went 'whoosh!' and flew to the floor.

"The man's wife was a little disturbed by that. Mildly freaked out." Beck reported. "Me being a skeptic, I asked the man, 'Well, were the windows open?' No. 'Was the air conditioning blowing across?' No. I put myself in her shoes. Maybe she saw this camera and sort of picked the paper up and threw it down. But I saw the video. There were other small things on the counter. They would have blown off, too. My conclusion, and I think, his conclusion, was that something made that piece of paper move. Maybe by the process of deduction, you could consider that that was our friend, the Pink Lady."

One time, two employees of the inn were standing outside the hotel that was closed and locked for the winter. They reported watching the lights of all the sixth-floor guest rooms come on at once, and then turn off abruptly.

Elvira Sanchez works at the Grove Park Inn on the Housekeeping staff. Stories about electrical oddities are not foreign to Elvira, as she has witnessed strange occurrences at the hotel first-hand. She knows that the spooks are not just stories.

Elvira reports that some guests feel as if they are kept in the closet by the Pink Lady. "The closet door is open, but they can't walk," Elvira said. "They feel something heavy on their shoulders."

"Stuff mostly happens at night," she continued. "One time, I was working second shift in the main building on the fourth floor. We were next to a pair of swinging doors and I felt something like wind on my back. My friend said, 'Oh my God! What is that?' When we turned around, the doors were swinging, going 'squeak squeak squeak squeak!'" Elvira squeaked and made a hand motion like swinging doors.

"The doors were moving like someone had gone through them?" I asked.

"Yes!" she said. "We try to run and we can't. We were there one minute, two minutes, who knows! We wondered, 'Is it still there?' We looked, but, no. It's gone."

Sometimes Elvira works in the Country Club buildings. She related a story to me from 2006.

"I was going with my team to clean," she said. "At night, we never go as just one person to clean up. We go as two or three. They were having a breakfast early the next day. We go and we are talking and cleaning. Then, it is time to go. They asked us, 'Did you turn the light off?' We said, 'Yeah yeah. Let's go.' There is nobody there. We got in the golf cart to go back to the main building and started to leave when we saw that the light was on! I asked my friend, Rosa, 'You turned the light off?' 'Yes!' she insisted. I pointed at the light to show her that it was on. Right when I pointed at it, the light turned off. I said, 'Oh my God!' And then, while we watched, it turned on again! I said, 'Oh no. We're out of here.'

"Some people say that they won't go there because they are scared. I'll go there by myself in the daytime." She offered.

"But, not at night?" I asked.

"Not at night," she confirmed.

An employee who has worked at Grove Park Inn for more than a year asked to remain anonymous, but, told me a tale of one night when he was working alone.

"Right now, I work in-room dining, but I used to work maintenance when I started here. One night back then, they told me to go down to the Country Club by myself to stack chairs. My supervisor had already left. At first, I was kind of scared because I was still new. I knew I was alone in there because I didn't see any golf carts out in the parking lot or anything. And, all the lights were off except in the one room where I was. I had made sure all the front doors were closed and all the exterior doors are closed. I was stacking chairs and had my music playing. As I was stacking chairs, suddenly I hear a loud bang, like a clatter of doors."

"It was the sound of a door slamming?" I asked.

"Yes, like the door slamming shut. I was just like, 'No, I'm not staying here!' So, I start stacking chairs fast to get out. When I got done, I started walking really fast up the hill. My supervisor drives by me and says, 'Did you see a ghost? You look like you just saw a ghost.' I told him, 'I think I was almost attacked by a ghost!'"

Another former employee worked in Security at the hotel. When making rounds at the Country Club buildings, she opened the door to one room and found all the chandeliers swaying! She left immediately. Another employee hated to set up for events in the Country Club. She claimed that spirits destroyed unattended floral arrangements, locked doors, and threw couch cushions onto the floor. Others claimed that the Club was haunted by a man in a bowler hat that caused elevators to malfunction.

Klara Hines is an employee at the Grove Park Inn who works in the Country Club buildings. Klara has heard numerous stories in the 19 years she has worked at the inn. She told me, "When I used to work at the pro shop, sometimes I would notice that somebody had walked in and so I would approach and say, 'Hello...hello?' But there was no answer and nobody was there."

One former Grove Park Inn employee named Jamie had his own brushes with spooks while on the job.

"I worked at Grove Park for a bit in the kitchen," he told me. "The kitchen was almost underground. They kept us away from the patrons. We were like crazy Morlocks to these people. Once, in a hallway, something said my name in my ear. But there's absolutely nowhere close in that hallway for anybody else to be. It freaked me out so much that I started walking off. Then I felt something hanging on the back of my hoodie, like a little pinch that I felt pull loose when I kept walking. There was nothing for me to get hung on! I was like, 'Okay. I don't really like that. Don't whisper in my ear like that.' Saying my name is fine. But whispering in my ear is a little spooky.

"One time they asked me to bus tables, so I go up to bring stuff down. They have a giant fireplace in there and, as I'm clearing dishes, I saw a red thing above the fireplace mantel. I saw it out of the corner of my eye. I thought it was a reflection. You know how a really bright light burns your eyes a little bit? That's what I thought I was seeing. So, I didn't pay attention to it. But I bent down and then I saw it again. The second time I saw it, I was like, 'Oh, shit. Okay, that's a thing. Let me look at it for just a second.' I stopped and I could see it. It was almost like a paint smear. But it didn't look pink. It was reddish, almost blood red. It was only a matter of seconds and then it faded away, like a match going out.

"I stood there for a second. A guy that was working with me was like, 'You saw that, didn't you?' I was like, 'Yeah.' He goes, 'That was Pink Lady.' I was like, 'What? What are you talking about?' He goes, 'Yeah, the Pink Lady comes up every once in a while. Usually it's bad.' I was like, 'Oh, that's just fantastic. Cool.' I quit the next day. I was like, 'I don't wanna be here with a bad omen ghost checking me out.'"

Another Omni Grove Park Inn employee named Mary had stories to share about things she has seen and heard, including the infamous Pink Lady.

"When I first started working here, I was in Housekeeping," Mary told me. "They sent me to 545 to clean the room because somebody had checked in and didn't like the room and checked out. I just had to go and make sure it was clean for the next guest. I was walking around and I straightened up the bathroom. I went around the bed to check it when I started hearing somebody in the bathroom, like clinking in the sink. I was like, 'Hello? Hello? Did somebody come in?' Nobody answered, so I got up and went in the bathroom. Nobody was there! I went back to the bed and started looking around and cleaning again when the noise started up again. I said, 'Somebody is playing a joke on me.' I went out in the hallway but there was nobody there. It was really, really weird.

"I went back to Housekeeping. I said, 'Something is wrong with that room.' They're like, 'What room did you go to?' '545.' They said, 'Ha ha! You met the Pink Lady!' I was like, 'Say what?' I did not know.

"I'll ask guests in the morning, 'How was your night? Was everything okay?' They would be complaining of knocking on the wall from 545. I'd go to the front desk and say, 'Hey, who is staying in 545 right now? Guests are telling me that somebody was knocking on the wall at 3:00 in the morning.' They're like, 'Nobody.' 'Oh. Okay. I'm not telling the guests that.'"

Later, Mary left Housekeeping to staff the elevators in the lobby. During these new shifts, she had a few encounters with the Pink Lady.

"I've seen the Pink Lady a couple of times up on the fifth floor, late at night," Mary told me. "One time I was walking around for exercise. Standing here all day, you get tired. As I was walking around in circles, this wisp of pink and blonde went right by me. I was like, 'There's nothing there!'

"Before they moved the front desk over here, it was over where the Model A car is now. I was operating that elevator, standing over there. All of a sudden, this light came over by the fireplace, hit the walls, and bounced into the elevator. I was like, 'That's weird.' I told myself maybe it was light from a car, maybe somebody opened the door. All of a sudden, the elevator door starts going like this..." Mary shook the elevator gate forcefully to demonstrate. "It didn't come off, but it kept shaking," she continued. "I got in and pushed five. I took whatever it was up to the fifth floor and I said, 'Don't bother me no more!'

"You might believe it. You might not. It hasn't done it lately, but that same elevator used to call you up to the fourth floor and nobody would be there. Dusty and I had to check it out. One night she was on the other elevator. I said, 'Dusty, if I call you on my cell phone, I want you to go up to the fourth floor and let me know if somebody is pushing the button. You know, cause kids will play tricks on you: push the button and run. I got a call and I told Dusty to go up to the fourth floor real fast. I got in and went to the fourth floor. Dusty said, 'Mary, there was nobody there.'

"If you ignore it and don't pay it any attention it will stop. You ignore it and wait until it buzzes again because if it buzzes twice, it's a guest. Then you go up and you'll see the guest. But that first time, if you answer it and go up to the fourth floor, it will bother you the rest of the night. It's weird!

"A while back, before they put the mountain terrace down there, that area was, at one time, the indoor pool. They had closed it down and filled it in with gravel. I went down to check it out and see what was going on. While I was down there, I saw a lady walk in the door. I saw her plainly. She had on a skirt that was down to her knees, a sweater, and boots. She looked like a regular person. I thought it was one of the coordinators so I went to say, 'Hi!' Then she vanished. I was like, 'Okay, that wasn't a coordinator. I'm going back upstairs.' That was the one and only time I've seen her.

"We had a guest staying up at the main inn and they had a little boy. He got out of the room and they couldn't find him. Security was looking for him and they caught him on camera down in the spa area. When they finally caught up with him. They asked him, 'What are you doing?' He said, 'This nice lady wants to show me her hotel.' There was no way he could have got out by himself because he couldn't reach the locks. They couldn't figure out how he did it. He also had a teddy bear on that trip and he lost the teddy bear. Everybody looked for it but couldn't find it. About a month later, they found the teddy bear down in the spa.

"I see shadows going through the walls every now and then, mostly in the back halls behind the meeting rooms," Mary explained. "You're like, 'Did I really see that shadow go through the wall?' You think it's just a play on your mind, on your eyes.

"If you go down to the Country Club, there's supposedly a man down there and he does not like us workers. He thinks he's better than us. If you are there real late and you're making too much noise, he would bang on the ceiling. Especially dishwashers, especially by themselves. It was very hard to keep a dishwasher down there. We used to only have one gentleman who would stay down there by himself at night and he was just brave.

"I have been down there. I would be standing in the kitchen looking past the ice machine and you'll see a shadow go down the stairs to the side of the kitchen. You're like, "Whaaat?" and you'll go check it out to make sure somebody else hadn't come in the room with you. But nobody's there.

"One time when I was by myself, I had an ice scoop thrown at me. Our manager, he's had things thrown at him when he was by himself. He's heard a ball bouncing and a little girl giggling.

"We used to have this girl that worked here and she was not afraid. She didn't believe in ghosts, but she was afraid of rats. She was always afraid she's going to come across a rat. One morning she had to work by herself down there at the Country Club. When her husband dropped her off, she's like, 'No, no, no, no! Come in here and make sure there's no rats running around before you leave.' As soon as they walked in, the chandelier started swinging. Then she was like, 'No, no, no, no! You're staying until the sun comes up.'

'We also had a Captain that didn't believe in ghosts and he was there late one night. He was coming down the stairs. Upstairs, it's nothing now but it used to be meeting rooms and the bridal room was up there. As he was coming down the stairs, the chandelier started swinging. He's like, 'Okay, now I believe all y'all's stories.'

"If I was there early in the morning, just me by myself, I could hear people whispering. And I was the only one there! Either I'd hum to myself to drown them out or I'd put on my earphones. It happened a lot. Constantly you would hear things.

"One morning I was by myself. I was coming out of the kitchen into one of the rooms that has bay windows looking out over the golf course. I saw a shadow of a man standing there and he turned around, looked at me and vanished. I was like, 'Okay, y'all leave me alone today!'"

One anonymous employee works at the Grove Park Inn in the PBX department, which is staffed with telephone operators that route calls for the resort. "I work nights, 10:00 p.m. to 8:00 a.m." he told me. "Working nights, I'm here through all the darkest of hours."

He confided to me that his favorite time to be at the inn is an unusual one. "It's not fun for the guests," he began. "But, my favorite time to be here at the resort is during a power outage or if they have to shut down the power to do some maintenance. Lots of times, this seems to coincide with the moon waxing or being full.

"When you walk down some hallways during those times, it is beautiful, like a photograph. The moonlight slants perfectly across the entire hallway. It makes alternating patches of light and shadow. In between the patches of light where it is dark, you really can't see anything in those shadows. It's eerie.

"I would walk down the hallway like that and think, 'This is the beginning of every horror movie!' That's how it starts and you're doing the thing that people do: you just keep going. But, it's one of my favorite times because it makes the atmosphere much more haunting and historic. Like you step back in time. When it was built, there was very little electricity, if any, here. Can you imagine the Great Hall area like that, where we are right now?"

He confides in me that he had a strange experience one night during one of his shifts.

"I get a few breaks during the night shift when they basically just let me walk around for a bit. One night, I went on break around 3:00 a.m. I typically walk up here to the Great Hall, I chat with people, move around, get the blood flowing so I can stay awake. Then, I was walking back to the place where I work. There's a registration desk area that's right there. And, next to that are some offices. They have doors on them that have...you know those narrow windows they usually have on school doors? With the lines in the reinforced glass? I'm just walking down that hallway. I'm approaching, but not really looking up. Something caught my eye in that instant. As I turned the corner and raised my head, I see something in the lower portion of that narrow little window in the door. My eyes directly catch the top curvature of a black shape. It looks perfectly like the size of a head. In the fraction of a second, I realized that I was seeing something. Then, as I watch, it ducks down.

"That, of course, makes me freeze for a few seconds! After 15 to 20 seconds, I'm staring at this door, thinking, 'Do I want open that? Did that just happen? I'm tired right now...is everything blurring out of proportion?' But it was a very defined shape. I peeked through the window as best I could and I didn't see anyone. Then, I opened the door to look around and double check to make sure. There's only two ways to exit from that specific area. That's either through the door I was looking through or through where I work. So, I went back there where I work and asked one of the night managers, 'Did you just go into that room there, for like half a second?' because she does have black hair. I thought that could explain it if I just didn't see her in that 10 to 15 seconds I waited if she ducked back in. But, she said, 'No, I haven't moved.'"

The employee has a theory about who it was that he saw. "From the height and the shape, I wonder if it's a kid," he said. "Like, a child that's running around and playing. Ducking down, maybe playing hide-and-seek? 'I see you, try to find me.' The other night shift operator says sometimes she can hear footsteps over there when no one else is in yet. If she leaves both doors open leading to it, she says she hears steps, like someone moving about in there."

With so many stories told for so many years, it is unlikely that the rumors about the haunting of the Omni Grove Park Inn will ever go away. Dusty the Elevatress has a theory about why hotels are often reported to be haunted. "A lot of times when people know they're going to die, they don't want to die at home. They want to go to someplace nice like a bed and breakfast, or a resort. That's probably why a lot of those kind of places are the most haunted."

However, Dusty thinks reports of spooky occurrences have become less frequent. "Guests don't report weird experiences as often as they used to. Maybe it goes in cycles," Dusty says. "I haven't felt the Pink Lady recently. I think she crossed over. She's a little mysterious, but she's a good soul."

Dusty also has a theory about the disbelievers: "I have a lot of guests who say, 'I don't believe it.' I tell them that if you are not open to it, it is not going to happen. You have to be open to it in order for this stuff to come to you."

You can visit the Omni Grove Park Inn to try to catch a glimpse of the Pink Lady and decide for yourself.

THE OMNI GROVE PARK INN IS LOCATED AT 20 MACON AVENUE IN ASHEVILLE, NORTH CAROLINA. CALL 800-438-5800 FOR INFORMATION ABOUT TOURS OR LODGING.

The Omni Grove Park Inn entrance

Undated photo courtesy of the Omni Grove Park Inn

The Palm Court at the Omni Grove Park Inn, location where the ghost known as the Pink Lady reportedly died.

Undated photo courtesy of Omni Grove Park Inn

Left to right: Thomas Edison, Harvey Firestone, Edwin Wiley Grove, Henry Ford, and Fred Seely at the Grove Park Inn

Photo courtesy of the Edward Ball Collection, Southern Highlands Center, University of North Carolina at Asheville.

Grove Park Inn grand opening banquet in 1913

Photo courtesy of Omni Grove Park Inn

Omni Grove Park Inn References

Bailey, Heather L. "Edwin Wiley Grove." *Tennessee Encyclopedia*. http://tennesseeencyclopedia.net/entries/edwin-wiley-grove/. Web. Accessed November 7, 2018.

Barnard, Bob. Interview with the author.

Captain Bob, an Inn employee. Interview with the author.

Cronin, K.C. "The Legendary E.W. Grove: A Man with a Vision." *Explore Asheville Convention & Visitors Bureau*. https://www.exploreasheville.com/stories/post/the-legendary-ew-grove/. Posted September 3, 2015. Web. Accessed November 8, 2018.

"Edwin Wiley Grove and Grove School History with Index." *E.W. Grove High School*. http://www.ewgrove.com/groveleg/ewdex.htm. Web. Accessed November 8, 2018.

"The Grove Park Inn Story." *Omni Hotels and Resorts*. https://www.omnihotels.com/hotels/asheville-grove-park/property-details/history. Web. Accessed November 7, 2018.

Hines, Klara. Interview with the author.

Horne, Beck. Interview with the author.

Hunt, Max. "Horror in the highlands: Asheville's ghostly legends provide a glimpse into city's past." *Mountain Xpress*. https://mountainx.com/news/horror-in-the-highlands-ashevilles-ghostly-legends-provide-a-glimpse-into-citys-past/ Posted October 27, 2016. Web. Accessed May 1, 2020.

Jamie, a former Inn employee. Interview with the author.

Joanne, an Inn employee. Interview with the author.

Neufeld, Rob. "Visiting Our Past: Old Battery Park Hotel yielded to new in 1922". *Citizen Times*. https://www.citizen-times.com/story/news/local/2017/08/06/visiting-our-past-old-battery-park-hotel-yielded-new-1922/534827001/. Published August 6, 2017. Updated August 7, 2017. Web. Accessed March 3, 2020.

The Omni Grove Park Inn. (2016, February 22.) *Brief History of The Omni Grove Park Inn* [Video]. YouTube. Web. Accessed November 7, 2018. https://www.youtube.com/watch?v=3xKDa1EKYyw&t=635s.

Mary, an Inn employee. Interview with the author.

Miss M., a former Inn employee. Interview with the author.

"The Mystery of the Pink Lady." *The Omni Grove Park Inn.* Flyer distributed by Special Events at Omni Grove Park Inn. Received November 7, 2018.

"The Omni Grove Park Inn - Historic Walking Tour." *The Omni Grove Park Inn.* Flyer distributed by Special Events at Omni Grove Park Inn. Received November 7, 2018.

Pappas, Dusty. Interview with the author.

Pappas, Steven and Guinn, Gina. "History Goes Bump In The Night. Grove Park Inn." *History Goes Bump in the Night.* http://historygoesbump.blogspot.com/2016/04/hgb-ep-117-grove-park-inn.html. Posted April 9, 2016. Web. Accessed May 1, 2020.

Sanchez, Elvira. Interview with the author.

Wikipedia contributors. "Edwin Wiley Grove." *Wikipedia, The Free Encyclopedia.* Wikipedia, The Free Encyclopedia. Web. Accessed November 7, 2018.

ASHEVILLE MASONIC TEMPLE

The Asheville Masonic Temple at 80 Broadway Street in downtown Asheville, North Carolina, is notoriously haunted. When I first asked around about haunted locations in Asheville, numerous people told me emphatically, "You have to check out the Masonic Temple." After investigating stories about the building, I have to agree that they are right.

When I first visited the Lodge, I was given a delightful tour of the Masonic Temple building by curator Mason Ron Lambe, secretary of the Asheville Masonic Lodge. He recalled the path that originally brought him to Asheville.

"I was born in Greensboro." Ron told me. "I lived in San Francisco during those halcyon years, '64 to '79. I've got a picture of me and Mayor Moscone. And Jim Jones. I felt like Forrest Gump sometimes. Then, work brought me to Asheville in 1988.

"I remember, in the late 1980s, downtown Asheville was boarded up, really. There was not a soul to be found on the street after five. It was dangerous. Just unsavory. But there have been several programs that opened up the downtown and now it is great! It is second only to Miami Beach for Art Deco buildings. The big boom here was in the teens and '20s before the crash came and stopped everything."

Ron detailed for me the history of the Masons in Asheville, as well as the history of the building. Though the temple building dates back to the early 1900s, the Mt. Hermon Lodge No. 118 actually began operating much earlier, in 1828. At that time, the Masons met in a log cabin in North Asheville that was owned by the Sons of Temperance. The Mt. Hermon Lodge was officially chartered on December 13th, 1848. With

107 members, they met in the Drummer Building above Smith's Drugstore on Pack Square.

Ron explained that, around that time, the Lodge membership exploded. "It grew so large and so fast, that by the turn of the century, they had seven or eight hundred members. They had to break it up. That's how we got three Lodges in Asheville: Biltmore, West Asheville, and the head, Mount Hermon."

At that point, they had to build a larger facility to accommodate the expanded membership. Ron explained, "When they decided to build this building, they considered this lot. There was a discussion that the property was 'too far out of town.' Asheville was small!

"They had to scrape together the funds to get this building built," Ron said. "It was not easy. They didn't have a lot of money." To complete the endeavor, the Mt. Hermon Lodge joined forces with the York Rite. Then, the Scottish Rite wanted to join in. Ron clarified, "Three bodies built the building: Mount Hermon, York Rite, and Scottish Rite. They were very separate. That was a big issue."

The downtown lot was eventually purchased on July 1, 1909. At the time, the street in front of the temple lot was called North Main Street, but is now known as Broadway.

In 1912, the Asheville Citizen reported that "Within a few months, the lot at the corner of Woodfin and North Main Street will be the site of one of the handsomest and most convenient Masonic temples in the South."

Planning meetings for the building design began on April 6th, 1912 with architect Richard Sharp Smith, himself a Mason, who came to Asheville originally to supervise construction of the Biltmore House. Smith also designed a home on Kimberly Avenue for attorney William Jennings Bryan.

"The meeting minutes are fascinating," Ron noted. "They go back to 1848 and talk about taking up extra collection money for candles. And, when electricity finally came in, they had to have a doctor approve that it was safe to use!"

Building plans included a basement and first floor that housed the lobby, library, offices, reading room, banquet hall, and kitchen. Originally, the temple basement included brass spittoons and a bowling alley! A small Lodge Room in the basement includes logs and saplings used in Masonic rites. The basement to this day contains wicker furniture that is older than the building itself, dating from their time meeting in the Drummer Building. The second floor would be used by the Blue Lodge and bodies of the American or York Rite. The third and fourth floors would be used by the Scottish Rite and were referred to as the Scottish Rite Cathedral.

Construction on the building began in July of 1913 when the cornerstone was laid. The granite foundation is two feet thick and a total of 600,000 bricks were used in the construction. The Masons finally occupied the building in 1915. In 1922, an Otis elevator was installed. All original plans, deeds and survey plats are kept in the temple's records.

The first-floor library remains an impressive collection. "The oldest book here in our library is from 1804," Ron said. "Another book refers to a national Mason's meeting, the triennial assembly, held in the actual temple here, Asheville, North Carolina, in 1921."

When I commented on the remarkable bookcases in the library, Ron told me they were part of Richard Sharp Smith's original designs for the building. "You'll see this vertical diamond pattern all throughout the building," he told me. "Almost everything in the building is original, including the glass in the bookcase doors." Original brass doorknobs on the first and second floor are adorned with the Square and Compass design, while third and fourth floor knobs display Scottish Rite Eagles.

The upper floors also included a theater with a horseshoe balcony and hand-painted backdrops for scenery. Those same original scenery drops are still in the theater and in use to this day. Despite their age, they are spectacular.

"Those are 100-year-old sets!" Ron exclaimed. "The scenery drops in the theater were hand painted right on the floor of the theater by Chicago artist Thomas Moses in 1915," Ron said. "There are 47 of them. About 25 scenes of temples, forests, and more, all tied to the Lodge stories. It is one of the largest collections. Nowadays, most Lodges just use projections."

Fellow Asheville Mason Lonnie Darr agrees. "Those backdrops are 115 years old and they're priceless. You cannot touch the drops with your hands. The framework to lower them uses lead weights and hemp ropes. It's all original! And, they are not curled. When raised, they hang, uncurled, fully upright up above your head when you're on that stage."

"There are some generic Masonic drops, but they were primarily made for the Scottish Rite." Lonnie said. "We don't use them too much.

For a few years, the Montford Players used them for their plays. They would come and use the stage during the Wintertime."

I mentioned that I had heard the Lodge had been rented to film part of the remake of the Dirty Dancing movie. "Yes! That's our theater!" Ron exclaimed proudly. "And, they respected the building and the sets."

The theater was also designed with a sweet spot. When someone stands in the spot and speaks softly, their voice is carried throughout the theater. "The ceiling is not flat," Ron explained. "It may look flat, but it is not, so it reflects the sound. This was amplification before electronics."

The seating in the theater is original, as well. "In fact, if you raise a seat and look, there's a wire thing underneath to hold your hat," Ron explained.

Near the theater is a wardrobe room. A well-preserved, ancient cabinet holds original costumes that date back to the earliest days of the Mason productions. Ron explained, "There are 32 Masonic degrees. A degree is a morality play that teaches a moral precept. Each is acted out using costumes and the backdrops."

"This was used for dances," Ron said of the historic dining room. It retains the original 100-year-old maple floors and light fixtures. Ron showed me a mirror that was originally from a historic downtown hotel that was torn down in the 1920s. One hallway displays portraits of all the Masters, including the first Master of Mount Hermon from 1848."

The building has three balconies for use by the Lodge members. The second and third floor balconies are covered, while the fourth-floor balcony is open air.

"In 1918, there was the Flu epidemic," Ron said. He explained that the temple building was handed over to the Health Department and the Red Cross. Part of the temple was specifically used as an emergency ward for women patients and African-Americans.

"All the restaurants were closed. Everything was closed!" Ron said. "They served 60,000 meals out of this kitchen. So, this place has a history of interacting with the community."

But, during the '40s and '50s, the Lodge building generally was not easily accessible. "You practically had to have a note from your teacher to get in here!" said Lonnie Darr. "But the building is very expensive to operate. And, the Masonic bodies just didn't have the resources to cover it."

Eventually, the three Lodges had a bit of a falling out over finances. "Scottish Rite wanted to sell the building, but, we did not. They were thinking of how much money they would make!" Ron declared. "But you could not replace this building. It was built using steel beams for $65,000. It's like a battleship! It's substantial. In fact, it was a fallout shelter during the Cold War."

Eventually, the Grand Master came in to settle the standoff. "He decided that the building could not be divided and if it was sold, that the money would go to charity. So, we opened it up and now we have rentals here." Ron said. "The building was designed by the Masons for Masonry and has ever been used as such. We've just added an extra dimension with the rentals."

The tour continued as Ron opened the doors to the Lodge room. It was truly breathtaking. It was at once beautiful and mystifying. "Am I allowed to be in here?" I asked. He laughed and said, "Yes." Ron explained that after the building had flooded, they had to repaint the temple and chose a more colorful scheme. Tall columns that were previously white were marbleized. The floor appears to be made of marble until you look closely and see that it is actually painted.

One exception is the area where an intricate walnut inlay depicts the Masonic symbols of a square, level, and plumb. An intricate globe depicts the earthly sphere and the heavenly sphere. It, too, is original from 1915 and still depicts the Russian Empire. All the light fixtures in the Lodge room are original.

I notice a decorative depiction of different types of columns.

"There's a lot here for education of architectural issues and lots of Masonry symbolism," Ron said. "All lodges represent an inner chamber of King Solomon's Temple and should be oriented due East. Churches are supposed to be that way because the Second Coming is from the East. But they don't really do that anymore. The altar should be in the East.

"Everything has a meaning," Ron explained. "The Master sits in the East, Senior Warden in the West and Junior Warden in the South. But, if you'll notice, there are no officers in the North. People can sit in the North, but no officers. Because in King Solomon's temple, the sun never came in the North side, so it is deemed a place of darkness. You want your officers to see what they are doing."

I was surprised when Ron told me that no atheists can become a Mason. "You have to believe in a higher power by any name. We honor all paths. It's not just a Christian path, but the Jewish, and the Muslim, and Dharti. We have one brother who was Cherokee and took his from the Corn mother. It's a higher power.

"Times change and mores change, but the values don't. Masonry is pretty steadfast," Ron asserted. "It's stayed that way since 1717. The roots go back to building the pyramids, you know."

I thanked Ron profusely for the tour.

"I do it every day! I love history and I love this building. We've lost a lot of the old Masonic temples," Ron lamented. "It's sad. And, we came close to losing this one. But you can't replace it. This building will be here a long time. Longer than me!"

I marvel out loud once more that the building is so well preserved, and Ron's reply speaks volumes: "It's because we love it."

Mason Lonnie Darr provided more details about the Lodge building. Lonnie has lived in Asheville since 1999 and joined the Masons in 2009. In 2013, he became Master of the Mount Hermon Lodge. Lonnie has spent a lot of time in the Asheville Masonic Lodge building and knows it inside and out.

"I just love that building," Lonnie told me. "Right now, there are three Masonic Lodges that are associated with the Asheville Masonic Temple," he said. "There is Mount Hermon Lodge, of which I am a past Master. There is Veritas Lodge. These are both Blue Lodges, being the Basic Masonry, which is the first three Degrees. And, also York Rite Lodge. The Scottish Rite used to be there," he added. "It even says so on the front of the building."

In recent history, the building suffered a tragedy when it flooded during a terrible storm in 2012. "The roof was in terrible disrepair and started leaking," Lonnie said. "There was tons of damage in the theater, but not one drop of water got on the scenery drops. The ceiling collapsed in the dining hall. The light fixtures hanging from the ceiling were full of water. In the Lodge room, just above, a whole section of wall collapsed. There were six inches of water on the beautiful hardwood floor in there. But the restoration company came quick and kept any permanent damage from happening."

"That's when they decided to start renting it out, to cover the costs of repairs," he explained. "We were struggling to make enough money to keep it up. It takes about $85,000 a year just for maintenance and upkeep."

Lonnie explains that the Lodge building is a great deal more than just a meeting place, more than just a location to rent for events.

"The building is a Masonic temple. One of the greatest Masonic writers, Albert Pike, writes that Freemasonry is an amalgam of all of the religions of the world and all of the mystic organizations of the world. The Kabbalah says there are 600,000 ways to reach the divine. Curious that the Asheville Masonic Temple has 600,000 bricks," he explained coyly.

"Masonry has its own mysticism and there's also a lot of mysticism that is assigned to Masonry," said Lonnie. "Everybody's heard of Masonic secrets. I say there are two kinds of secrets in Masonry: There's the secrets that are myths made up by people who weren't Masons and there are the real secrets. But some of it is real. A real secret is something that cannot be revealed because it lives in the heart of the members. Truly, there are few."

"Masons are a mysterious crew," Lonnie admitted. "People say, 'You guys have so many secrets!' Well, we're a fraternity. Do we have a secret handshake? A secret word? Guilty. But, beyond that, not really."

"I used to give tours of the building a whole lot, almost every day," he said. "People would say, 'We know that you guys are trying to take over the world.' I would get weird questions all the time. I had a woman ask, with all sincerity, 'Is that the altar where you sacrifice virgins?' I said, 'Oh, no. We stopped that decades ago.'" I laughed, but worried aloud about his revealing too many secrets of Masonry in our interview. "It's like knowing God," he explained. "You can't know Him in his entirety, but you can know a little bit here and there. Masonry is the same."

I asked him about the rumored secret tunnels under the Lodge building. "There are stories of tunnels under Asheville connecting to our building. In that regard, I can neither confirm or deny," he said with a wink. "There are stories of the children of members playing in the tunnels."

Joining the ranks of the Masons is more straightforward than I expected. Lonnie said, "We can't invite people to be Masons. They have to ask. But I've heard some incredible theories, like you have to be specifically invited to meet in a dark alley in the middle of the night and then a bag is pulled over your head and you are escorted somewhere. I wondered, 'Where did you hear this stuff?' It is true that you cannot be an Atheist and be a Mason. You have to believe in a supreme power, in one great creator. We don't care if you say Jesus or Allah or Buddha or what."

Lonnie points out that several of the founders who signed the Declaration of Independence were Masons. "To say that Masons had something to do with the beginnings of our country would be a big understatement. The idea of democracy began in Masonic Lodges in Europe, where members all voted on what happened. That was a totally different concept. These ideas grew up under the monarchs, but it happened without the monarchs seeing it, in the Lodges. It is against Masonic law to discuss politics or religion in the Lodge room. We're no different than anybody else: everybody has opinions about everything. But we don't fight about it. And, generally speaking, our ears and hearts and minds are open to spirits running up and down the stairs or doors being opened in the middle of the night or lights coming on in the third-floor bathroom. We don't pooh-pooh that because there's lots of great things that happen in that building."

Lonnie knows about strange goings-on in the Asheville Masonic Lodge building better than almost anyone alive. In 2009, he found himself spending a great deal of time in the building, both during the day and at night. While there, he began to have some strange experiences that he could not easily explain.

I asked Lonnie if he had ever had any brushes with the paranormal before he spent time in the Asheville Masonic Lodge building.

"I have had strange experiences before," he confirmed. "Not bad. But I have felt spooked. Mostly in places that were not my home. Like, I would wake up and hear the bed creak. I'd be sure somebody was sitting on the bed, but nobody was there. I would always ask myself, 'Am I wide awake?' Yes, I'm wide awake."

After joining the Asheville Masons, Lonnie began to have unusual experiences in the Lodge building.

"Lots of interesting, unique things happen in that building," Lonnie told me. "And, I have had many weird things that happened to me there. But everything that happened in the Lodge had a benign feeling to it. There was nothing scary. It always felt like a good thing, like somebody was playing. It was weird, but I was totally comfortable with them!" he confided. "I felt no threat or anything like that."

Eventually, as Lonnie spent more and more time at the Lodge building, he had more and more strange experiences.

"I had just become a Mason in January of 2009. I joined the Asheville York Rite and they needed a secretary. I was an exceedingly lousy secretary, but they needed one and I stepped in. As such, I had an office on the second floor, which is where the Lodge room is located.

"I started living there six months later. I was going through a divorce and I was there a whole lot. I was spending 16 to 18 hours a day there, every day, mostly at night. I was there from noon until 4:00 in the morning. This was from about the middle of 2009 to the middle of 2011.

"In the Lodge room, there are lots of things that are just strange," Lonnie admitted. "It's a beautiful room. In the far right-hand corner, there's an exit door that goes up to the fire escape. Several members of the Lodge report that, when they go over near that exit door, they become very nauseous. To this day, when they go into that corner, they get nauseous.

"I was telling stories about the building to one of the people that I coached when he became a Mason. He said, 'It's funny, there's a place in the Lodge room that makes me violently nauseous.' I asked him where that was. When he told me it was that same spot, I said, 'I'm not surprised.'

"After we started talking about it, other people started to come forward to say, 'That happens to me, too!' So, I don't know if it was the power of suggestion, but I believe these people. They're not people who would exaggerate these kinds of things."

Lonnie then mentioned Joshua Warren, an Asheville ghost hunter and member of the Mount Herman Lodge.

"Joshua Warren and his crew used to do a ghost tour of the building and they would use equipment to look for things. He uses RF (radio frequency) detection devices and magnetic meters. They would set up their laser lights going all over the room. Supposedly, if there was any cloud or apparition that appeared, it would help them see when it was caught in the lasers. One night, a group of about 16 elderly women came in for the ghost tour. I knew this was happening, but I wasn't in there with them. I was in my office. Joshua took them in and sat them on the right as you walk in the Lodge. They turned the lights off. Everybody was sitting in the dark and it was very quiet. I was the only other person on the whole floor and I was at the other end of the hall. They sat there for quite a while, then Joshua stepped out to go to the bathroom. While he was in the bathroom, we heard all the women scream!

"He came running back and turned on the light in the room from the switch, which was out in the hallway. He ran in and asked, 'What's going on?' The women explained that while they were sitting quietly, they were surprised to hear, 'RAP! RAP! RAP!' from the front of the room." Apparently, in the darkness came three loud raps of a gavel on the podium at the front of the Lodge room, near where the Master sits. The women rushed up there to look around behind the Masters podium and under his chair. They examined everything closely, but didn't see anything.

"Of course, they were thrilled! You hear about people going on tour after tour...only rarely do you ever hear of anything happening. They go on this ghost tour and, suddenly, this happened! I was at the other end of the hall, so I missed it. But I heard the screams."

Lonnie takes a pragmatic approach to trying to understand these types of experiences.

"I have a scientific background," Lonnie said. "I'm an electronics engineer, so I look at this stuff as, 'How could this be explained?' I always look at those things with a grain of salt because there may be an explanation. But there have been some anomalies that are hard to explain."

For example, during the wee hours of the night when Lonnie stayed in the Asheville Masonic Temple building, he heard and saw things that he simply cannot find a rational explanation for.

"Now, I'm a Marine, so, security is a thing," Lonnie disclosed. "When I'm there, I always walk around the building. I always knew the doors were locked. I always knew everything was closed up. Some people, it freaks them out to walk the building in the dark. To me, it was fun. I enjoyed it and I had no problem with it. I know the building extremely well. I've been in every corner, in the attic, on the roof.

"One night, it had to be 2:00 in the morning. I was there and I knew that nobody was in the building. I went in the bathroom on the second floor. In that bathroom, one wall is right beside the stairwell.

"I'm sitting in the bathroom and on the other side of the wall, I hear THUMP THUMP THUMP THUMP THUMP down the stairs! It was real fast, like somebody running down the stairs. Like a little kid would. Not the kind of sound that an adult would make on the stairs. Then, they ran on down to the first floor. And, then they ran back up again!

"When I left the bathroom, I searched the building bottom to top. Through the basement, third floor, everywhere. Everything was still locked up. Nothing had changed. That was the first time that happened. I thought it was pretty interesting."

It turns out, this was not a one-time scare. The spooks in the Masonic Lodge have a distinct preference for waiting until Lonnie is in a bathroom to start with their antics.

"Another time, I went into the basement bathroom. The basement itself can be spooky. It bothers some of the Masons, anyway. I was in the bathroom when I heard somebody running down the stairs. Then, I could hear them in the hallway outside. There were no sounds of chatter or anything like that, just the sound of footfalls. It sounded fast, like a child or children. That bathroom was also near where the elevator comes down in the basement. At the same time, I heard the footsteps, the elevator engaged."

Lonnie was mystified, not only because he thought he was alone in the building, but also because the elevator is very old and has peculiarities to get it to operate.

"The elevator was put in in 1922," he told me. "It's all manually operated. It doesn't go anywhere automatically. You can't hit a call button from another floor.

"I knew that the elevator was on the second floor earlier and that I had closed the doors in the elevator. You can leave them open and the elevator won't go anywhere. But I had closed the elevator doors on the second floor and afterward, I went up and down using the stairs. That night, I heard the kids running on the stairs and I heard the elevator come down to the basement."

"When you came out, did you go see if the elevator was actually down?" I asked.

"I did!" he answered. "The elevator was actually down there."

Another time, a spook made its presence known in a bathroom on a higher floor.

"When I stayed there, I would be there all night with nobody else there. I'd have all the lights off in the building except for my office.

Before I'd leave for the night, I would turn off my office light and go all the way up to the fourth floor in the dark. I'd walk around and check everything. Occasionally, when I would come back down to the third floor, the bathroom light would be on! So, I would look around all over the third floor and check around the building again. Finally, I'd turn the light off. When I'd get done, it was 4:00 in the morning and I was ready for bed. But when I'd get down to the parking lot, the light is back on in the third-floor bathroom! So, I would go upstairs. I'd turn on the lights. I'd look through the building again. I'd turn everything off. And, when I'd go back to the parking lot, the light is back on in the third-floor bathroom again!

"Each time I went up there, the switch was actually flipped to 'On.' It wasn't a malfunction in the wiring. This whole thing happened to me on four or five occasions. In fact, many people over the years have noticed that third-floor bathroom light turning back on."

On one occasion, Lonnie was surprised to find that the ghost seemed to attempt to be helpful, for a change.

"One night, I left the bathroom nearby to my office. As I came back into my office, I realized I'd left the light on in the bathroom. I said out loud, 'Oh crap! I left the light on.' I turned back, and as I grabbed the bathroom door and opened it, the light went out! I checked the switch and it was flipped to 'Off.'"

Like any respectable haunted building, the Masonic Lodge also has stories about doors opening and closing on their own.

"When I first became a Mason," Lonnie began, "The Master of the Lodge told me, 'There are lots of things that happen in this building. Not bad things. Just strange things.' He told me to keep my eye on the third-floor balcony. Late one night, the building had been locked up for hours and hours. Sometimes, I'd sit on a couch on the third floor in one of the theater dressing rooms. That night, as I sat there dozing in the wee hours of the morning, I was awakened by a really cold chill."

Because it was cold outside that night, this prompted Lonnie to get up and check the nearby balcony doors.

"There were two doors that go out to the third-floor balcony. I knew they had been closed and locked up tight. Like, physically latched. But I got over there and those doors were wide open. These aren't locks that can work themselves loose. Somebody would have to lift it up. And, those doors make noise! They're old doors that close tight, so they are hard to open and make noise when you open them or close them. But there had been no noise. I thought someone must be in there and I searched the building. But there was nothing. And, I'm not the only one. A couple of other people have said that they closed and locked those doors, but when they came back later, they found them open."

Sometimes, a spooky event is not centered on lights or doors that seem to have a mind of their own. Sometimes, it is something that cannot be seen at all. Lonnie recalled the time something invisible scared one Mason right out of the building.

"One of the strangest things was when a Masonic brother visited from Johnson City, Tennessee. He had some work to do in Asheville that would last only three or four days. Instead of getting a hotel, he asked to stay in the Masonic building and we gave him permission.

"The first night there, he had a blanket and pillow and was sleeping on the couch in the lobby. It's not dark. There's a big window with street light coming in. The closest bathroom was in the basement. During the night, he got up to go down to that basement bathroom. He got halfway across the floor toward the stairwell and ran into something that stopped him in his tracks. BAM! But, as he looked, there was nothing there! He can see just fine and there was nothing there! He ran back to the couch, sat on it, and pulled the blanket up over his head. When he left the next day, he said he would not stay there again. He told me, 'I'll get a hotel.'"

I asked Lonnie if he had any theories about why the building might be haunted. He said he couldn't be sure.

"At one time, a girls' school was being built across the street, where the bank is now," he said. "Before the school was finished, they had no place to go. So, we let them use the building for classes. Nothing bad happened then that I'm aware of. And in 1918, during the flu epidemic, we housed overflow from the hospitals. We haven't been able to document whether anybody died in the building then. Chances are pretty good, but we can't verify that. We don't really know."

"There used to be a caretaker for the building who only had one arm," Lonnie recalled about Scottish Rite secretary, Herbert Noble. "He had also once been a butler at the Biltmore estate. He sewed all their garments, one-handed! He lived up on the fourth floor of the Lodge and died in the building back in the '60s."

It is hard to determine who may now remain of the numerous souls that have spent time during their lives between the walls of the Asheville Masonic Lodge building. But, one thing is for sure. People who spend time there these days are sharing quarters with someone who isn't letting go of the past.

"In terms of, 'Are these ghosts in the building? Are there things that happened in the building so people are meant to stay there? Are their souls still walking the halls?' I don't know," Lonnie admits.

It is fascinating that many paranormal events reported in this location happen to people over and over in the same way. Many have reported hearing children running up and down the steps. Many have reported the same lights going on and off. Many have reported feeling nauseous in the same corner of the Lodge room. But, in order to know that many people are experiencing the same strange event, someone has to be the brave soul who speaks up first to report that it happened to them.

"Nobody talks about it at first," Lonnie said. "But, after one person speaks up, then more people come forward to say, 'This happened to me, too.'"

Lonnie keeps a philosophical attitude about the strange events at the Lodge. "There's a Masonic prayer that says 'How filled with awe is this place and we did not know it?' Part of the awe of the Lodge is experiencing things like the kids running up and down in that building. Nothing has ever gone on there that scared me. There's strange things. And I lift my eyebrows and go, 'Wow! That was interesting!'"

THE ASHEVILLE MASONIC TEMPLE IS LOCATED AT 80 BROADWAY STREET IN DOWNTOWN ASHEVILLE, NORTH CAROLINA. IT IS A PRIVATE LOCATION, BUT TOURS CAN BE ARRANGED BY CALLING THE MASONIC OFFICE AT 828-252-3924.

Asheville Masonic Lodge Hall with exit door where members become nauseous.

Asheville Masonic Temple Opening Banquet (April 26, 1915)

Photo courtesy of Asheville Masonic Temple

Conclave photo at the Asheville Lodge entryway (July 1928)

Photo courtesy of Asheville Masonic Temple

Asheville Masonic Temple References

Lambe, Ron. Adapted from research by Carroll Melton. "Asheville Masonic Temple: A Brief History." Flyer distributed by Asheville Masonic Temple.

Lambe, Ron. Interview with the author.

Lonnie Darr, Lonnie. Interview with the author.

Wikipedia contributors. "Asheville Masonic Temple." https://en.wikipedia.org/wiki/Asheville_Masonic_Temple. Web. *Wikipedia, The Free Encyclopedia.* Accessed November 7, 2018.

REYNOLDS MANSION

Woodfin, North Carolina, is the location of one of the oldest pre-Civil War brick homes in Buncombe County: the Reynolds Mansion. The Reynolds Mansion is a two-story, double-pile brick home built in 1847 by "Colonel" Daniel Reynolds with a team of 15 enslaved laborers. Reynolds had the majestic home built for his wife, Susan Adelia Baird Reynolds, on a 1500-acre plot of land that was gifted from Susan's father. It included woods, farmland, and apple orchards.

Over the next 30 years, Daniel and Susan Reynolds raised ten children in the home: five girls and five boys. When Daniel Reynolds passed away in 1878, the home and remaining 140 acres of land was inherited by his son, William Taswell Reynolds. On October 6, 1880, William Taswell married Mamie Elizabeth Spears and they raised four children.

The home and land were sold in 1890 to William's younger brother, Nathaniel "Natt" Augustus Reynolds. Just two years later, in 1892, William died at the age of 42. Ten years later, in 1902, widow Mamie Spears Reynolds married her former brother-in-law, Natt. It was during this time in the early 1900s that Natt remodeled the Reynolds Mansion to have a more Colonial Revival style, adding a kitchen, wrap-around verandas, and a third story with a dormered mansard roof.

In 1919, the home was leased to Dr. Elizabeth Smith who operated a 16-room osteopathy sanatorium there. Patients were treated for various ailments during the height of Asheville's status as a top destination for travelers seeking to better their health.

Dr. Elizabeth Smith had the distinction of being the first female physician in Asheville at a time before the 19th Amendment to the Constitution granted women the right to vote. Smith became the first president of the Asheville Business and Professional Women's Association, which was a non-partisan social and networking group for women pioneers of the professional community.

One of William and Mamie's children was Robert Rice Reynolds, born on June 18, 1884. Robert was known as "Our Bob" during his career as a United States Senator from 1932 until 1945. In the 1930s, Natt and Mamie moved back into the home and helped raise Senator Reynold's children by his first wife, Frances, who died of typhoid fever when the children were toddlers.

Senator Reynolds was ultimately married five times. He met his third wife, a French woman named Denise D'Arcy, when he struck her with his truck as she crossed the street in New York. Five days later, they were engaged. One year later, they were divorced. Next, he married a Ziegfeld Follies dancer who later died of tuberculosis.

Senator Reynolds was married in 1941 at age 57 to his fifth wife, 19-year-old mining heiress Evalyn "Evie" Walsh McLean. Evie was the then-owner of the famed 45-carat Hope Diamond which was insured for $250 million. Evie was known to loan the gem out to local brides for their weddings. Evalyn and Senator Reynolds' only daughter, Mamie Spears Reynolds, is rumored to have once buried the jewel while playing in her sandbox.

 In 1946, Evie's mother made the gruesome discovery that Evie had died of an overdose of sleeping pills, which some attributed to the curse of the Hope Diamond. Mamie, who was only four years old when her mother died, would have inherited the gem, but believed it was what killed her mother, so her father instead sold it to famous jeweler Harry Winston in 1949. The gem has been displayed in the Smithsonian since 1958 on permanent exhibition.

At age 19, Mamie Spears Reynolds became the youngest car owner in NASCAR and the first woman to qualify for the Daytona 500. She also owned the Kentucky Colonels basketball team and her godfather was J. Edgar Hoover.

After Mamie Elizabeth Reynolds died in the '40s, daughter Adelene Reynolds Hall returned to live in the mansion with her father, Natt. Adelene had married Lawrence Hall who ran the Hall Coal Yard and the mansion was referred to as the Hall House during that time. Their three children were named Natt, Margaret, and Annie.

When Natt Reynolds died in the 1950s, daughter Adelene inherited the house and subsequently passed it on to her daughters, Annie and Margaret. It was a remarkable feat that from 1847, one family had maintained ownership of the home. The house was not sold out of the family until the early 1960s.

In 1970, the home was sold to Fred and Helen Faber. When they acquired it, it became evident that time, the elements, and neglect had all taken their toll on the mansion. Rainwater leaks had extensively damaged the home. Woodwork was falling apart. Undaunted, Fred and Helen remodeled the mansion, doing all the work themselves, including modernizing the kitchen. In 1972, the work was complete and the Fabers opened the mansion as a Bed and Breakfast called The Old Reynolds Mansion.

Fred Faber died in 2003, but Helen continued to run the Bed and Breakfast until 2008. When the work became too much for her, she shut down the inn, and the mansion was once again abandoned to disrepair.

Luckily, in October of 2009, Michael Griffith and Billy Sanders purchased the Reynolds Mansion from Helen Faber, intending to restore it to its former glory. The dilapidated house and overgrown grounds needed extensive repairs. It was not until April of 2010 that the Reynolds Mansion began operating again as an opulent Bed and Breakfast.

Over time, bathrooms were added and the kitchen remodeled, but the basic structure of the house remains very much as it was when Daniel built it in 1847. The mansion now sits on four acres, a historic island at the center of the Reynolds Village development. The Reynolds Mansion was listed on the National Registry of Historic Places on September 13, 1984.

I spoke with a local Asheville resident (who wished to remain anonymous) about her spooky experience at the Reynolds Mansion. I asked her if she was a believer in the paranormal before her experience there.

"It's not that I wasn't a believer," she replied. "It's just, I didn't think ghosts existed. I'd grown up Episcopalian, so, it wasn't that I didn't believe or did believe. But, for me, ghosts, as in, dead people who still have some kind of presence here on this Earth, I definitely did not believe in. I would say I had a very normal, middle class, 'ghosts don't really exist' kind of upbringing."

I asked her when she visited the Reynolds Mansion.

"In 1994, I came with someone to the Reynolds Mansion for a special occasion celebration, but pretty spur of the moment," she told me. "It was in July, and July in Asheville is always rockin' at Bed and Breakfasts! They only had one room left which was upstairs on the third floor, the corner room. And, that is a gorgeous, old mansion. Being from Western North Carolina, I knew a lot of things, but, hadn't really done the 'Bed and Breakfast scene' in Asheville and didn't know anything about it. The person I was with was from Asheville and they did know a fair amount about the town. We go and everything was wonderful."

"When you checked in, did you notice any hesitation or did they mention anything?" I asked. She responded that she was not forewarned.

"That's what you will come to discover was so funny about the whole ordeal. Nothing was said about it. I didn't know anything about it, other than it was a cool, old, big, house, this Bed and Breakfast. I think it was fairly late evening when we arrived, so, we didn't really mill around a bunch. I think it must have been a Friday, late evening. We were gonna do stuff that weekend.

"For houses of that age, the servants' quarters were on the third floor. When they turn them into a bed and breakfast, the bedrooms are a little room with the space taken up in the room itself for a small bathroom. So, the bathroom was in the room, but it was enclosed. The bed was right beside the bathroom.

"As Fate, or luck, would have it, the person I was with fell asleep instantly and is a very sound sleeper. I'm not. It takes me quite a while to get to sleep. And I'm very sensitive to sounds. The bathroom was an enclosed room, but the door was open. I heard a noise coming clearly from the bathroom that sounded like water running. Like the sink was running or the toilet is broken. Because I was laying on that side of the bed near the bathroom, it wasn't six or eight feet from me.

"I sat up thinking, 'I just need to go jiggle the handle or turn the faucet off.' But, when I sat up, the sound stopped! I thought, 'Okay, that's cool. I didn't have to do a thing.' I laid back down and the sound started again! I can't remember how many times that happened, but it was three or four or five.

"I don't know how ghosts are actually able to do what they do. How could he sense when I was getting up, and stop? I didn't even have to get all the way up and it would stop. And, I varied the times! I laid there and said, 'I'm gonna wait a longer time', or, 'I'm gonna do it instantly.' But it was almost instantaneous that it would stop.

"I thought, 'Okay, there's no spy camera. There's no trick going on in here,' where every time I would get up to go see this noise and fix it, it would stop very quickly. Then, suddenly, I knew someone was in the room.

"It was the strangest thing, being a non-believer and you suddenly go, 'Someone is in this room and they didn't come through that door that is locked.' I knew it was a ghost because you just know. I knew immediately it was a male. You'd might say 'Well, how could you know?' But, it's as though you and I are sitting here talking. You're a woman and I knew this ghost was a man. Then, the presence moved!

"It moved from the bathroom or it could have been in the corner of the room. He moved to the end of the bed. It's not that I saw his form, as though I can tell you 'tall' or 'short', 'lean' or 'heavy', or what color hair. I can tell you it was a man's presence and he moved to the end of the bed. It was July, so it was hot and the window was open. Then, the presence went out that window. And, when he was out the window, he made a noise that was completely otherworldly. A very bizarre screech or scream, but almost in a comical way, like if someone was trying to imitate a cat. But it was clearly up high. I've had cats all my life and it was no cat."

"This all happened very quickly, within a couple of minutes of the original water noise. I said to myself, 'Okay. There was just a ghost in this room. It was a man. And, he left by the window. And, he made a bloodcurdling, bizarre sound.'

"Then, there was some kind of strange peace that came with it. I didn't feel I'd been threatened. I didn't lay there and panic. Or have any fear. I didn't wake up the person I was with. I didn't run downstairs and panic. Just intense shock and curiosity. I laid there in philosophical contemplation. Then, I went to sleep.

"Of course, once he left, the sound never came back. The bathroom never made another peep. Not another noise! I just accepted it as something that opened up a whole different mind thought process for me.

"The next morning, I told the person I was with, 'Well, you're not going to believe this. I didn't wake you up because he was already gone, but there was a ghost in this room.' He didn't flinch. He said, 'Yeah, this house is haunted. I didn't want to tell you about it. People have known about the Reynolds Mountain ghost forever. He has haunted the house for a very long time.'

"I was like, 'What did you say?' I was just stunned! We went downstairs and asked the owners about it. They said, 'You know, we haven't heard from him in a while!' They had all these newspaper clippings and stories and books, the whole nine yards! I was flabbergasted, honestly. But I felt like I was some kind of guinea pig since I was not a believer and didn't know about it.

"I'd grown up in Brevard, which is 45 minutes away, so I'd never heard about it. I'd never heard about hauntings or a mansion. So, it wasn't like a self-fulfilling prophecy: 'Oh let's go stay at the Reynolds Mansion and we'll get lucky and this ghost will come.' For me, it was anything but that. I'd never heard of it, never knew about it. And probably, if I had, I wouldn't have believed it.

"In the days and weeks that followed, it did begin to haunt me. Not 'him,' but, the thought that I had to accept that it really happened. I'm a very skeptical, practical person. The more I thought about it, the more I'd come back to it. I couldn't change the fact that it had happened and that I knew it was a ghost. I couldn't talk myself out of it. I couldn't explain it away.

"Those first weeks and months afterwards were strange. I went through a period of stages you go through when you've actually been with a ghost. It started getting a little scary for me. I'd be home at night and it would be dark and I'd think, 'Okay, how would I feel if a ghost came in here and it wasn't a friendly ghost? You start thinking all these 'What ifs'. That movie, The Sixth Sense, came out right about then. That was very difficult for me to watch.

"It's obviously been quite a few years since then and I've told friends about it. It's very interesting when you accept it for what it is. At that time, I was still living down East, so, I was way far away from Asheville. Totally out of sight, out of mind. But things would come up, like the movie, and you'd have to think about it. I thought, 'I just want to forget about this,' but I've had to accept it. As time goes by, you hear other people tell their ghost stories or you read about them. The good thing is, most ghosts, I think, are not aggressive. They're not mean, evil spirits that can actually do something. I do think that once you accept it, you have to wonder, 'Are they going to know that I know about this and come see me?' And, when that doesn't happen, you return to a peaceful phase where it is what it is. It's pretty amazing. It is still hard to wrap your head around. What does it mean? What is that space that these people are occupying? It's fascinating."

I spoke with the then owner of Reynolds Mansion, Billy Sanders. He recalled the events that led him and his partner, Mike, to live in Asheville at the Reynolds Mansion.

"In Chicago, Mike and I had corporate jobs and we hadn't told any person that we were looking into a Bed and Breakfast, except for Mike's aunt, Claudette, who was our realtor here in Asheville. Mike and I had narrowed down the potential BnBs to four. We had a neighbor who was a spiritualist. She always frightened me. Every time she would see me, she'd ask, 'Are you doing okay?' and I would wonder if she thinks I'm gonna die!

Mike wanted to test her abilities. He said, "I told her, 'I want you to look at these four pictures. Tell me what you think of these houses.'

"She said, 'This one right here is not what it seems, not what you think it is.' She was talking about the Wright Inn in Montford.

"'This one here, I don't feel comfortable. A lot has happened here, not good things.' That was Albemarle Inn.

"Then she looked at Abbington Green. She said 'I don't have a yay or nay about this one. It's just kind of blah.'

"Then she said, 'This one, there is a spirit here on the third floor. There's a lot of activity here.' She was looking at Reynolds Mansion.

"She asked me, 'Are you thinking of opening this as a BnB?' Me and Mike, we both couldn't believe it! We never said a thing. But she knew it just from looking at the picture of the house. So, it was meant to be. I was meant to be the caretaker of Reynolds Mansion.

"When we came to Asheville, we originally were going to buy an inn that was up and running. Reynolds Mansion wasn't an inn at the time. It had been shut down for years and was in very bad disrepair, in terrible shape. I remember when I first saw it, even as bad a shape as it was in, it had a really good feeling and aura about it. I remember walking in and it had such a neat feel to it. And, it carries that feeling even today that impacts a lot of people. We purchased Reynolds Mansion in 2009."

Billy told me, "When we were looking at it, we knew it was reportedly haunted. But it didn't bother me. I remember asking the lady we bought it from, 'I've heard that it's haunted,' and she just kind of smiled. I remember telling Mike, 'She's afraid we won't buy it.'"

"They dug the bottom of Beaver Lake for the clay to make the bricks to build this house," Billy said. "It took three-and-a-half years to construct. It was 1500 acres when it was built. All of Reynolds Mountain, all the way to the French Broad River, and all the way to Beaver Lake. It was all apple orchards. The Senator had them all cut down when he inherited it. He didn't want to be an apple farmer.

"It's nice to be the caretaker of it," Billy assured me. "Most people, when they come here, are taken aback with just how large it is. The website doesn't do it justice. You can't capture the scale and size of it. You know, it has the second-largest dining room in Asheville after Biltmore! When they walk in, there's so much to see. They are overwhelmed and don't even think about ghosts.

"I've never been a big believer in all of that," Billy assured me, "But, I've learned a lot through the years. Now, I've never seen anything myself, but I have seen the effects of it. The thing I notice most about Reynolds Mansion is a lot of mirrors. And, mirrors reflect paranormal activity. If you ever see anything, that's where you'll see it. In the mirrors.

"That grand foyer mirror has been here since the house was built. It was bolted into the bricks by the slaves who built this house. It has reflected every person who has walked through the doors of this house. I don't ever look in it when I come downstairs! Generations of the Reynolds family lived here from 1847 until 1972, which is a long time for one family to live somewhere. They had a lot of trials and tribulations. It's interesting what the house records about their life and allows you to see as you live in it. I feel a lot of it is like static electricity. It's energy that is built up over time. At certain times, and because of certain people, that energy expresses itself.

"There have been many people come through that have that ability to see things and they know immediately. I'll have guests come up to me and ask, 'Do you ever have any problems here?' and I'll say, 'What kind of problems?' They say, 'I'm very sensitive to the paranormal and I felt it immediately when we checked in.'

"Every morning, I sit at the table with my guests and they have a lot of questions about the house and the history," Billy explained. "The first time it happened, there was a man here with his wife. After breakfast, he came back in the dining room while we were clearing the table. He said, 'I just want to tell you that while you were talking at breakfast, there was a young woman standing by you that was trying to get your attention.' Well, I went back in the kitchen and told Mike, 'He is crazy as a bedbug!' Because I'd never seen anything. But it wasn't six to nine months after that, there was a young girl from Russia here. She sat at the very end of the table and couldn't speak very good English. After breakfast, she came up to me and she said, 'When you talk, there's a young girl standing by you trying to get your attention, doing this on the table.'" Billy pantomimed someone tapping on the table. "That was two people from two very, very different walks of life."

"When I lived in the main house, there have been many, many times you could hear people talking," Billy said. "That I would hear a lot. All the time. Or, you would hear someone talking in the house when there would be nobody here. You couldn't quite understand exactly what they were saying, but they were having a conversation. One of the things that will happen is the skeleton keys for the doors to the rooms will lock. Either you will hear them lock, or guests will come back and can't get in their room.

"When we lived on the third floor, we would let out our two English bulldogs. When they would get to Annie Lee's room, they would raise their head and start wagging their tails. My hair would stand up on my arms!

"One time it was late, about 10:00. I was watching TV in our room upstairs. The doors were shut and no one was here. The dogs were laying on the floor. All of a sudden, the door just shook. The dogs jumped up, barking! I didn't think 'ghost,' I thought, 'Oh my God, somebody's in the house with me!' I threw the deadbolt on the door and I just stood there. The dogs eventually calmed down. I finally got brave enough to slide the deadbolt back. I opened the door and stood behind it to let the dogs go out into the hall. But there was nothing there. I tell you; somebody had a hold of that door and shook it."

Billy described for me the time he had an experience in the Maggie room that he could not explain. He made the bed in the room and then walked out. Shortly after, he returned to the room. There, on top of the bed he had just made, was an old, rusty hairpin. He had no explanation for where it had come from. No one had been in the room in the interim and no guests were registered to the room at the time.

A woman that once stayed in the Maggie room complained that the door to the room would not stay shut. The first night, she locked the door with the key she'd been given and got in the shower. After her shower, she was startled to discover that the door to the room was open. Later, she contacted the daughter of a friend, whom she knew had also stayed in the Maggie room before. Upon asking if she had any trouble with the room, the lady promptly said that the door would not stay shut! Over time, it seems this was a common complaint for guests staying in that room.

Other guests complain that their keys go missing in the Maggie room. Most times, they would mysteriously reappear under the bed, even after the area had previously been checked. Another guest registered to the Maggie room had just gotten in bed when she felt a tug on her sheets. While wondering if her imagination was playing tricks on her, the sheets were tugged *again* and moved up, as if to tuck her in.

"You learn that it's just part of the house," Billy said.

People tend to think the spirit being seen and sensed is Annie Lee Reynolds.

"Annie was the only Reynolds daughter of the five girls that never married and she lived here till the day she died," Billy told me. "A historian told me that they think that she died of tuberculosis.

"One guest had checked in and only been up to the carriage suite. They hadn't been back to the house because they had dinner reservations and then went on to bed. But, after breakfast, she said that, in the night, she had woken up to see a tall, slim lady with her hair up. I asked her if it was frightening and she said 'No!' that it didn't bother her at all. I showed her a picture of Annie Lee. She said, 'Oh, that's her. She was just standing in our bedroom.'"

Annie's bedroom, now called the Maggie room, is on the third floor.

"Sometimes, guests see Annie Lee just as clear as day," Billy said. "I've had people see her in her room, sitting. And, in the kitchen. And, in the dining room. One time, I was in the kitchen. A woman had gone up to Annie Lee's room. She came down and she said, 'Do you ever have any problems with the room on the third floor?' It took me aback that she knew that. I said, 'That was Annie Lee Reynolds' room. That bed was hers and everything. People see her.' She said, 'Oh yes, she's here right now. She's setting there in that chair.' I said, 'You see her?' She said, 'I do! She's wearing a paisley dress and her hair is up. She is not aware of me.' I thought that was very interesting.

"Usually, you see her on the staircase. There's a picture of Annie Lee standing on the stairs, and it's in color! You can see the sun come right through her. It really is amazing.

"Somebody saw her standing in the front hall! Two women were wanting to see about hosting a baby shower here at the mansion. I was out in the yard, so they had to come around back. They asked about having the shower here, I said 'Well, we're not even open yet,' because we were still in restoration. They mentioned that when they were knocking at the front door, they saw the woman standing there in the hall. I asked them what she looked like. They replied, 'Oh, she's very beautiful and her hair was up in a bun.' They described Annie Lee to a T. I said, 'Well, I'm the only one here.' But they both saw her."

I asked Billy if the women were freaked out.

"No, they were actually very calm," he told me. "I have learned in ten years of running this place that either people have that ability or they don't. When they have it, they have dealt with it their whole life and they are very calm about it. To some people it's a little bit of an irritant. Like they don't know how to shut it off.

"I have a feeling that Annie Lee is around me more than I know. More than I even care to think about," Billy admitted. "Guests have seen Annie Lee over many years. But, if a guest comes and experiences things and they don't even talk about it, we never know."

I asked Billy if he found that guests are often seeking a spooky experience at the inn or if more people are turned off by the idea.

"Do some people come here just for that? Yes, they do," he confirmed. "But, not as much as you would think. I tell people, if you have not ever seen anything, the odds are you probably will not. Because you have to have that ability. I've never had anybody scared to stay here. We've never had anybody who has been nervous about it. Usually, the people that do experience something, they didn't come here for that. And, when they do, they are not blatantly like, 'Oh my God, I have to tell you what I saw!' They are actually very calm and very matter of fact."

"They actually feel lucky," said Sandy Hatchwell, the Manager at Reynolds House, joining our conversation.

"Sometimes, a guest will come and set this house into disarray," Billy told me. "We recently had a lady here who was almost like a charging rod."

"We knew it was her," said Sandy. "She told me she was a medium. She was a lovely lady, but she did stir things up a bit."

"It intensifies, it does," Billy agreed. "Nobody's cameras were working. Nobody's phones were working. The music wasn't playing. The lights were blinking. And, it was her! One guest had a very, very expensive camera. He thought it was broken. But then everybody started saying that their phone wasn't working. I thought, 'There is something going on here.'

"It can get bad. Sometimes it will last for two-and-a-half weeks! When you've got a whole full house of guests here, it's an irritant. I was very glad when she left. I told Sandy that I would not care if she doesn't come back!

"When you have a lot of guests, you have more of a chance for somebody that has that ability," Billy suggested. "I think I noticed it more in the house when I lived here. That's why I wanted you to talk to Sandy because Sandy has lived here two-and-a-half years. When you're in here at night by yourself, you know how it feels, you know how it smells, you know the sounds," Billy nodded towards Sandy, who agreed.

Billy explained, "There was a woman here that was very sensitive who said this of the energy in the house: 'It's a very healing feeling.' It's interesting that she chose that particular word with this house having been an osteopathic sanitarium, which would have been very hospital-like. I told her that people believe it's Annie Lee Reynolds. She said, 'Oh, it's more than one. It's many.'

"In 1920, Nathaniel Reynolds leased the mansion to the first female physician in Asheville. Her name was Dr. Elizabeth Smith. She ran this house as a sanitarium for tuberculosis for about five years. So, a lot of people lived and died here. One of the guys that a lot of people see is a tall, slender man, usually on the third floor. He has a beard and looks like a physician."

One time, an employee polishing a mirror in the Vera guest room saw behind her in the mirror's reflection a tall, thin man with gray hair. She turned to ask if she could help him, but then the man wasn't there.

Billy gestured to a bookcase in the room.

"There's actually a doorway behind this bookcase," he said. It was a door between the library, where we were seated, and the Lila guest room next door.

"But you can't keep that door locked!" Billy insisted. "I have got newspaper articles from the '60s that says they would try to deadbolt the door but it won't stay locked. When we bought it, Mrs. Faber told us, 'That door's not gonna stay locked.' Well, I didn't believe that. We rented that room, but guests would say 'That door opens up in the middle of the night.' Well, we can't have that! So, we backed up a bureau on the other side and put bookcases on this side. When Daniel Reynolds comes into this room and people see him, he is usually standing here. I think he's wondering why the bookcase is there."

One guest that stayed in the Lila room appeared at breakfast with an unusual tale. She claimed that during the night she saw a tall, elderly man. At first, she thought she was dreaming, but he told her that he was upset that the door in the corner of the room was locked. This guest had no idea about the door behind the dresser leading to the library that would not stay locked on its own.

"Sandy was here in the library reading and he walked into this room," Billy said.

Shocked, I asked Sandy if, when she saw Daniel, did he look normal or filmy.

"He is not at all filmy," Sandy confirmed. "He's very real. He looks like a solid person. But he is not of today's age. He's dressed differently, he holds himself differently, and he is totally unaware of me. It's like he is not even seeing me. A lot of times he is standing right there by the bookcase. Only once he was in the bedroom where the doorway is. He doesn't look confused, he's just standing. I'll be reading and look up and he's gone. The air in here changes--it feels different. But I never feel nervous and I never try to communicate or take pictures."

"We had a girl here that was a medium," said Billy. "She was going through the house and came into the kitchen. She said, 'There's a young girl in here who is telling me that she was embalmed here.' I said, 'Really?!' After she went out, Mike asked me, 'Why didn't you say something to her? You know all about that.' The only thing I knew was that Nathaniel Reynolds owned the funeral home on Woodfin Street, which is now Morris Funeral Home. William Morris, who was William Taswell Reynolds' great-great grandson, called me when he was 80 years old. He said 'I saw the restoration of the house on television. I remember being there as a young boy and seeing the Senator out on the porch smoking a cigar and plotting what he was going to do in Washington. I remember seeing Evalyn wearing the Hope Diamond right out there in the courtyard. My grandfather used to help Uncle Gus run the funeral home. That's what they called Nathaniel, was Uncle Gus.' I told him what that girl said about someone being embalmed here. I asked him, 'Do you know of them ever doing that on Reynolds Mansion property?' He said, 'Oh, Hell, they used to embalm them out there in the old garage.' Which is where I live now! This was the 1800s. Back then, there weren't the laws there are now."

I asked Billy what was the frequency for people to have a paranormal experience here.

"It's interesting what people see and what they feel here," he replied. "I've often wondered if there's a pattern to it, but, there's not. If you had a graph, it would be up and down. You may go a long period of time with nothing. Then, all of a sudden you may have it for a long time. And, you may get a guest that has that ability, and it will start and stay for a long time."

"Some people think you will only see activity at night, but oh, no, no. Uh uh," Sandy assured me. "Spirits are around us at all times."

"If a house is haunted, it's haunted all the time," Billy agreed.

"One time I remember, there was no one here," Billy recalled. "Sandy was in Colorado. We didn't have any guests. I had come in to the house and into the dining room. One of the dining chairs was pushed all the way against one of the walls. I just walked through and pushed it back under the table, then went on in and worked. When I got ready to leave, another chair was pushed all the way to the wall. I remember thinking to myself when I saw that first chair, 'I wonder what this is?' And, when I saw the second one, I thought, 'Oh God! Here we go!'"

I asked Billy and Sandy if there was a type of occurrence that people report more than anything else. At the same time, they said, "Orbs."

"Orbs can be all over in the house," Billy assured me. "We've had many guests see that." Billy showed me an impressive video of an orb that was filmed in the house.

"One gentleman had never had an experience and he just couldn't understand it," Sandy related. He and a lady came in the dining room and both saw an orb. "She had her phone in her hand and took a picture of it. He saw it with his own eyes, not in the picture! He said, 'I'm forever changed.'"

"Have you read Micah Hanks' book, *Reynolds Mansion: An Invitation to the Past?*" Billy asked me. "He had a seance here. I did not participate in that. But, during it, the electricity just went wild! We've had two paranormal investigations. The best one was done in 2011 by Joshua Warren. Josh told me that there are not many places that you see full body apparitions, but Reynolds Mansion is one of them.

"I remember telling Joshua that I'd never seen anything. He said that really doesn't mean anything. He said it could be that you don't have that ability or it's not meant for you. Or, you're too busy!"

Billy recalled what Joshua told him: "'There's a lot of theories about paranormal activity, Billy. One of them is the theory of parallel time. That the past, present, and future are always simultaneously going. But, every once in a while, they'll 'blip' into each other. And, that's what you're seeing, that blip. You aren't actually seeing a spirit; you're seeing a replay.' You know the feeling of déjà vu? Twice it has happened to me here. Once, I was going into the parlor and when my foot hit the parlor floor, that's what it felt like. It seemed and felt different. The air feels different. And, it looked different for just a moment! The second time it happened, I was going upstairs. When my foot hit the landing of the second floor, the same thing happened to me. And, these were months and months apart. That sensation lasted for just a little bit of time."

Billy speculates that what he experienced was one of these 'blips' in time. "I remember thinking to myself, 'Is that what I'm experiencing?' It's an odd feeling and you notice it when it happens to you."

Billy has made his peace with the residents of the house who aren't moving on.

"Sandy knows a lady who keeps wanting to come here and do a cleansing," Billy said. "I told her, 'Don't bring that woman to my house! I don't want them doing anything!' It is what it is and it doesn't need cleansing. I've never had anything bad happen here.'"

"People get a bond to this house and it's a very strong bond," Billy explained. "Even today, I get a call or email from people from other countries who say, 'You know, I can't get that house out of my head.' You almost feel akin to the house. It stays with you. It really does stay with you."

Rick Fletcher is very familiar with the Reynolds Mansion because he has stayed at the mansion as a guest many times over the years.

"The owners have really done a wonderful job restoring this house," Rick said. "It's just a wonderful house. I hope it's always preserved because it's a landmark. The previous owners, Helen and Fred, were wonderful people. They restored it in part, but never entirely. Helen wouldn't sell to the developers. She saved the house and about an acre and a half of land."

I asked him what originally brought him to the Reynolds Mansion. He told me that he lives in Virginia, but, visits Asheville for business and pleasure.

"We've been here every year since 2003, except one year when it was closed between the change of ownership. So, I've stayed in this house many times."

Hearing this, I suggested he was a true expert on the mansion. "I don't know if I'm an expert," he said, "but, I do have a lot of data points. I've had quite a few experiences in this house."

Rick's scientific reply was in keeping with his background. "I'm retired now," he said. "I've got a Masters in Computer Science and I taught at MIT for many, many years," he told me. "Prior to that, I earned a Master's degree in psychology. I have a B.S. in Biology. So, it's all sciences. I'm very much an analytical person. I am a rational, pretty analytical guy."

Rick's experience with the house dates back even further than 2003. "The first time I stayed here was in 1993," he told me. "A friend and I were in town and I didn't actually know Asheville at all. She said she knew of an inn and it was her idea to stay here. It was actually rather spontaneous. I think she never stayed here before. I had heard nothing about the house, no background at all.

"We stayed in the room upstairs on the third floor that is now used by the innkeeper. It was a rental room at the time and I remember it was green. It was an active night. I woke up pretty abruptly at about 1:30, 1:45 a.m. She was holding onto me and saying, 'There's something in the room!' In the room, I saw...let's call it a 'darkening'. Whatever it was, it went over the bed, across from left to right, and lingered over the bed, which was uncanny. It was really tense as it hovered over the bed. My friend was terrified. Then, it went across to the window and out of the room. We heard the shutters on the outside of the house rattling. But there was no strong wind to speak of that night."

I asked Rick if the experience was scary for him.

"It was a very strong experience," he replied. "It was the most unsettling of my encounters. But I wasn't terrified. I didn't feel a risk of any harm. At the time, I had the strong impression of it being a woman. And I did not know the history of the house.

"In the morning, in the dining room, I talked to the old owners, Fred and Helen. Fred asked me what happened and I told him. I probably should not have brought it up in the dining room at breakfast with other guests there. He didn't want me to be so forthcoming about it. They weren't wanting it to be leveraged since it was not a draw for customers. That was 25 years ago this year."

"Clearly, you weren't so turned off that you never came back," I suggested.

"No," Rick said. "I was curious about it. Plus, this is a wonderful house. The innkeepers are nice people. And, I like to know the stories of the places where I have experiences like this. But I would not be here again for ten years. I was here next in 2003.

"In the interim, I got married. We came to Asheville for a music camp and needed a place to stay. I thought of Reynolds Mansion, not necessarily because I was drawn to have more experiences. But I was curious about it and it was a nice place to stay in Asheville. Upon returning, I chose to stay in the same room where I stayed originally. Later, we did stay in Annie's room, which is now called the Maggie room. We've stayed in the Maggie room twice.

"Over 10 years ago, I saw my strongest apparition of Annie in that room. I remember it well. I was in bed and woke up about 4:30 in the morning. Early, early morning, but not dawn yet. I was awake. A slightly dreamlike state, but awake enough. The apparition was pretty clear and in full color! She was in her mid- to late 20s, young and very beautiful. Usually, she is spotted with her hair up. But, when I saw her, her hair was down. It was long and auburn. She wore a long, dark green dress. She was standing over the bed and initially not looking at me. There was an intrinsic sort of light source to it. I won't say it glowed, but that isn't far off. It illuminated itself. She was moving, as if in a slight breeze, from left to right. Then, she stopped. Her head turned and she made eye contact. It lingered for about a half a minute. Then, at once, it was gone."

At this point, I expressed to Rick that I would have been frightened.

"I had some anxiety," he admitted. "But, it wasn't scary. I wasn't afraid for harm or anything. It was uncanny. Very electric and very charged. It was more than eye contact. It was a mental contact of some kind. It was a consciousness. I can't prove it, but I'm positive she was aware of me. I think it made her anxious, and yet attracted, because we were aware of each other. I think the locus of it is here in this room, her room. Because this was home for her.

"In the morning, I went to Helen and said, 'Helen, I had this very strong apparition. It was so clear that I would like to look at some photographs.' She was skeptical and gave me a look. Right out there in the hall is what she showed me. It's a picture of Annie Lee and her four sisters. I picked out Annie Lee. It was very easy. I said, 'There she is!' Helen just said, 'You're right. That's her.'

"That was the first time I saw Annie Lee and the strongest apparition. And, the clearest! Clear as a bell. I mean, it was almost like a film. And, after that, every time, it's the same. Almost like a mental signature. I know it's her consciousness.

"I have seen Annie Lee once in a place that she has often been spotted, at the landing right outside the Maggie room," Rick continued. "She was white and wispy. She was not real bright, smoke-ish bright. Not moving."

"Could you tell what she was doing?" I asked him.

"She was looking down the stairs," he responded.

"Looking down towards you?" I asked.

"Yes," he confirmed.

"Another time, we had stayed in the Maggie room and were packing up," Rick began. "It was in the daytime, in the morning with a lot of light. The door to the Maggie room was closed, but when standing in the hall, you could see a bit of light from the room under the door. As I watched, a shadow went across that light. It blocked it. So, I opened the door. Nobody was there.

"I had another experience when we were staying in the Maggie room. I woke up, again about 1:30 or 1:45 a.m. I was in bed and my wife was asleep. The air was extremely charged. Then, the covers on the bed moved up! Just slightly, more over me. I felt like it was Annie. Her psychic signature, if you will. Her presence was very strong and right over me. Right around me."

"Did that keep you awake?" I asked.

"A little bit," he admitted. "I said, 'Annie Lee, I'm tired and I want to go back to sleep now.' And it stopped. In the morning, I told the owners about this experience and they said, 'Well, this has happened before.'

"I have an old friend here that's a native of Asheville," Rick related. "We went up to the landing right outside the Maggie room and stood awhile quietly. The lights began to flicker! Now, it's old wiring so it might be a short or a drop in the voltage. We can't prove anything. But the timing was very good!" Rick laughed.

Since Rick has stayed in numerous rooms at Reynolds Mansions, he has many reports of activity that he has experienced.

"One time we stayed in the Lila room," Rick said. "This experience was not like all the rest of them. It was at night and I was in the bed. I suddenly felt myself rising up off the bed. Very slowly being pulled up, just a little bit, over the bed. And, then I go back down. It was strange!

"Another time we stayed in a room on the second floor. In the morning, I heard a child crying. A high sort of crying. It wasn't loud, but it was there. It lasted about a minute. I've heard that other people have had a child actually appear to them.

"We stayed in the Henry room three or four times. In the Henry room, it would always be charged. I never had a jolting sort of encounter, but it was always a very strong presence in that room.

"We've also stayed in the carriage house. Billy told me that nothing had ever happened in the carriage house before," Rick said. "We like the carriage house because it's a little more private and more space. About two or three years ago, I was here to work on an album and rehearse and stayed in the Hydrangea room. I woke up at night again and I thought,

'Annie Lee Reynolds.' That happened every year we stayed over there. The last instance was two years ago. It was a lot stronger.

"In the morning, I remarked about it to Billy. Billy gave me an interesting look and told me that the couple who stayed in the adjacent carriage house room that night reported that they experienced a woman who sat on their bed. And, from how they described her, it was Annie Lee Reynolds.

"Billy said that's never happened before and he accused me of 'drawing her over there.' I said, 'Not intentionally!'"

"The Linda room is also pretty active," he said, "And, it's not only Annie Lee in that room. I'll wake up and there will be more than one presence in that room. Once, I perceived a collection of orbs over the bed that started to resolve into faces. Very faint, wispy, and smoky. Never distinct. It lasted just a few minutes.

"Another time in the Linda Room, I woke up at night to go to the bathroom. Again, probably about the witching hour: 1:30 or 1:45 a.m. I remember walking into the bathroom. Then, a strong presence came into the bathroom through the ceiling right over me and sort of lingered there. The air got very thick. It was a palpable darkening and a heaviness."

I told Rick that I was horrified by the idea of a ghost hovering over me in the bathroom at night.

"It's hard to explain why I'm not freaked out by it," he agreed.

The scientist in Rick has questions about these encounters.

"I'm curious," he said. "There are other people who've had a lot happen in this house to them, too. So, it's as 'real' as it can be because the activity has been repeatable. It is a mystery that we don't understand quite yet, but it has to be energy. There are people, there are times, there are occasions, there are experiences, when the levels merge a little bit. You get a window there. What really interests me is the fact that it's not just a static movie where an image recurs. It's an awareness. At least in Annie's case, there's something else that lingers here and apparently is not ready to move on. Annie Lee is the strongest presence in this house, for me. I've often wondered when she died. What hour? Maybe it was 1:45 a.m. Maybe she's really happy here. But I think she knows she's trapped. I hope that she is going to move on."

Rick found a unique way to commemorate his experiences at the Reynolds Mansion. Around the year 2011, Rick channeled his experiences and enthusiasm to write a piece of music inspired by Annie Lee Reynolds. "I recorded it and it's on the album I released late last year, *Taking Flight*," he told me. "The last track is called 'Annie Lee's Waltz'. The idea is that she waltzes alone in the house."

Rick's frequent stays at Reynold Mansion are not likely to end anytime soon, despite the occasional creepy events.

"It's a pleasure to be back here over and over again," he said. "It's a happy house overall. It just has a lot of charged energy. It's active, but it's not harmful. When you look out of the corner of your eye in this house, you'll have movement. It has me very intrigued about Annie and this house. They just linger here for whatever reasons. This house is fascinating and this story should be told."

Even today, the ghosts of Reynolds Mansion are compelled to interact with the guests who stay there. Billy and Mike sold the Reynolds Mansion in 2019. The current owner reported to me an incident that had occurred recently.

"About two weeks ago, we had guests staying in the Claudette room. The first night, they seemed to be having a great time. We have a wine pantry in the dining room and guests can help themselves. On the second evening, they were having a glass of wine outside upstairs on the upper porch. They came to chat with me and the man said, 'Honey, do you want to go and get us a glass of wine?' She said, 'Sure' and disappeared to get the wine. When she did, the man whispered urgently to me, 'I have to ask you something!' I answered, 'What? And, why are we whispering?' I thought maybe he wanted to book another stay for them, but he didn't want her to know. He said, 'Have you ever heard of any kind of...activity?' I asked what kind of activity. He whispered, 'Like, paranormal stuff.' I said that I'd heard of stories being told about paranormal activity in this house.

"The man whispered, 'Have you ever seen anything?' I told him I haven't. He didn't believe it! 'Really? Never? Nothing?' I replied, 'Fortunately, or unfortunately, not.' I didn't have an opinion one way or another. 'I've heard other guests make mention of it and ask questions,' I admitted to him. 'Why do you ask?'

"The man launched into his tale. 'The first night, I slept like a baby. But, last night, I woke up just before 2:00 a.m. and I heard a conversation going on. In the room. At first, I thought, 'Perhaps she is having a dream.' But she was sound asleep. It definitely wasn't her. Then, I thought perhaps there are other guests out on the landing upstairs. But I looked. There was no one out there. And, the conversation continued!'

"I asked the man what the conversation was about, but he didn't know. I asked him how did he feel about it. 'A little weird,' he whispered in reply. 'I thought it was a little creepy.'

"I asked him what happened next. 'Then, they stopped,' he replied. I asked him if he had felt threatened or in danger, and he said 'No. But then, I couldn't sleep.'

"I've stayed in that room before, the Claudette room," the new owner told me. "But I never had anything happen. I've stayed in all the rooms except Inez and Maggie."

I had to ask, "Are you avoiding the Maggie room?" He claimed not to be.

When Rick considers his experiences with the paranormal, he tempers his knowledge of science with philosophy.

"It has to be based on energy," he reiterated. "Some things are static like a movie that just repeats over and over again because it was so traumatic or powerful. But I think here are cases when it's more than that. When there is a consciousness that is aware of us. It really interests me how and why that works that way.

"It makes a lot of us uncomfortable to talk about it because if I talk about it, then I'm gonna be looked at as disturbed, or worse. People will say it's not happening, you're making it up. But, it's real. It happens over and over again to multiple people. It raises questions about afterlife which I think are very interesting questions. Having these experiences is unusual, but it's not abnormal. It's normal but not talked about, normal but not understood. We have to have some euphemism to talk about these things we don't know about. So, the expression 'paranormal' is used. One day, it will be normal. It will be explained. We don't understand the mechanisms yet. We are not yet at that state. But, we will."

Reynolds Mansion

Reynolds Mansion is a private location. Call 828-258-1111 or visit www.thereynoldsmansion.com for information about lodging.

Photo purported to be the ghost of Annie Lee Reynolds

Photo courtesy of Billy Sanders/Reynolds Mansion

Reynolds Mansion entry stairwell and original mirror bolted to the wall during the home's construction

The ghost of Annie Lee Reynolds is seen in the area of these stairs.

The Lila Room at Reynolds Mansion

The dresser hides the door that will not stay locked or shut and a ghost is sometimes seen standing in this area in front of it.

Reynolds Mansion dining room

Photo courtesy of Billy Sanders/Reynolds Mansion

Evalyn "Evie" Walsh McLean in 1914 wearing the Hope Diamond

Photo courtesy of Billy Sanders/Reynolds Mansion

Reynolds Mansion References

Fletcher, Rick. Interview with the author.

Hanks, Micah. (2012) *Reynolds Mansion: An Invitation to the Past*. Print. CreateSpace Independent Publishing Platform. Pages 17, 22-23.

Hatchwell, Sandy. Interview with the author.

"History of the Reynolds Mansion." *The Reynolds Mansion Bed and Breakfast Inn*. https://thereynoldsmansion.com/reynolds-mansion-history/. Web. Accessed May 2, 2020.

Hunt, Max. "Horror in the highlands: Asheville's ghostly legends provide a glimpse into city's past." *Mountain Xpress*. https://mountainx.com/news/horror-in-the-highlands-ashevilles-ghostly-legends-provide-a-glimpse-into-citys-past/. Posted October 27, 2016. Web. Accessed May 1, 2020.

Milling, Marla Hardee. "Reynolds Mansion reflects antebellum grandeur in Asheville." *Citizen Times*. https://www.citizen-times.com/story/life/home-garden/2017/11/10/reynolds-mansion-reflects-antebellum-grandeur-asheville/830430001/. Published November 10, 2017. Web. Accessed May 2, 2020.

"The Region's First Female Doctor and the Reynolds Mansion." *Town of Woodfin*. https://www.facebook.com/townofwoodfin/videos/vb.391071497624437/1159901704210356/?type=2&theater. Town of Woodfin Facebook Page. Posted on October 2, 2019. Web. Accessed on March 10, 2020.

Robinett, Kristy. (2014). *Forevermore: Guided in Spirit by Edgar Allan Poe*. Llewellyn Publications.

Sanders, Billy. Interview with the author.

Wikipedia contributors. "Reynolds House." https://en.wikipedia.org/wiki/Reynolds_House_(Asheville,_North_Carolina). Web. *Wikipedia, The Free Encyclopedia*. November 7, 2018.

Wikipedia contributors. "Robert Rice Reynolds." https://en.wikipedia.org/wiki/Robert_Rice_Reynolds. Web. *Wikipedia, The Free Encyclopedia*. November 7, 2018.

BATTERY PARK HOTEL

The downtown Asheville, North Carolina location of the Battery Park Senior Apartments has been the site of not just one, but two hotels named Battery Park Hotel. Its prime location on one of the tallest hills in the city has provided magnificent views for decades.

The land was originally purchased in the 1680s by Dr. Daniel Coxe, the physician to King Charles II and his court. Coxe referred to the area that ran from the Atlantic to the Pacific as "Carolana." This property was inherited by his son, Colonel Daniel Coxe IV. After Coxe IV moved to America, the onslaught of claims against his "Carolina" lands became insurmountable and he released his claim in exchange for 100,000 acres in New York.

The family was somewhat redeemed in 1795 when Colonel Daniel Coxe's grandson, Tench Coxe, bought half a million acres in Western North Carolina. Tench's son, Francis Sydney Coxe, established his family on their Green River Plantation, located south of Rutherfordton. It was in this home on the Green River where Frank Coxe was born in 1839. Frank Coxe, later known as Colonel Frank Coxe, paid $6,160 on October 1, 1885 for the land where he would site his soon-to-be-famous hotel.

The hill that Coxe chose for the location of the hotel was known as Battery Porter Hill because, during the Civil War, Asheville's Confederate defenders placed cannons there. Thus, Coxe was inspired to name his hotel Battery Park Hotel.

This first Battery Park Hotel was designed by Philadelphia architect Edward Hazlehurst in the Queen Anne style. The hotel boasted three stories at a height of 125 feet and stood on a plot of 25 acres. It opened for business on July 12, 1886.

At a time when most Asheville streets remained muddy and unpaved, the new hotel was a modern marvel utilizing telephones, electric lights, and Otis elevators. Each of the 500 guest rooms had its own fireplace. Paired with the fact that Asheville was one of only two American cities utilizing electric street cars, the city seemed the height of sophistication.

This new hotel became the center of social life in Asheville. Notable guests that visited the hotel included presidents Grover Cleveland and William McKinley, as well as the Rockefeller and Vanderbilt families. New passenger trains also brought an influx of people to the Asheville area mountains, including many seeking treatment for tuberculosis.

The hotel hosted its first wedding on Jan. 31, 1889, joining a Savannah railroad clerk with a Battery Park Hotel telegraph operator. In 1890, it hosted the Swannanoa Country Club ball. Arthur Murray's dance education tour also made lengthy appearances.

In 1903, The New York Times referred to the Battery Park Hotel as "one of the most perfect resort hotels in America. It is beautifully furnished and admirably managed. Its enormous sun parlor, overlooking the Balsam Range, is one of the most charming rooms imaginable. It has long stretches of glass-enclosed verandas on each floor.... It is homelike and cheery in every nook and corner. Its table is of the best, and the service of the house is up to the metropolitan standard."

Asheville native and famed author Thomas Wolfe described the Battery Park Hotel in his semi-autobiographical book, *You Can't Go Home Again*:

> "George could remember its wild porches and comfortable rockers, its innumerable eaves and gables, its labyrinth of wings and corridors, its great parlors and their thick red carpets, and the lobby with its old red leather chairs, hollowed and shaped by the backs of men, and its smell of tobacco and its iced tinkle of tall drinks.... George could remember, too, the smiles and the tender beauty of the rich men's wives and daughters. As a boy he had been touched with the unutterable mystery of all these things, for these wealthy travelers had come great distances and had somehow brought with them an evocation of the whole golden and unvisited world, with its fabulous cities and its promise of glory, fame, and love."

For almost forty years, the original Battery Park Hotel was Asheville's most notable landmark. Colonel Frank maintained a small residence right next to the Battery Park Hotel until his death in 1903.

In 1921, the Battery Park Hotel was purchased by Edwin Wiley Grove, who had recently completed the nearby Grove Park Inn. Grove claimed that he intended for the hotel to remain a resort for winter and summer months, but that did not come to pass. Grove's real intention was bringing downtown Asheville into the modern world by building a world-class hotel. On November 28, 1922, that the *Asheville Citizen* newspaper announced, "New 200 Room Commercial Hotel to Replace the Battery Park; Begin Developments at Once."

In December of 1922, Grove began excavation of Battery Porter Hill. As Rob Neufeld wrote in the *Asheville Citizen Times*, "The 10-acre plot was active with steam shovels, African-American workers, mules and pans, plus steer and wagons to cart dirt to Coxe Avenue. Streets were being widened to allow for parking."

The old Battery Park Hotel finally closed for business on September 15th, 1923, and demolition began shortly after. Contemporaneous reports in the news indicate that the hotel was purposely dismantled to be sold off piecemeal. Doors, windows, flooring, elevators, electric light fixtures, marble, brick, and stone were among the salvaged hotel items listed for sale in a 1923 advertisement. That November, Asheville paper *The Sunday Citizen* reported that a fire sparked from an exposed wire in an elevator shaft and caused $30,000 worth of damage to the old building. And with that, the once magnificent hotel literally went out in a blaze of glory.

Moving forward with his plans for the new hotel, Grove hired New York architect William Lee Stoddart to design it. Stoddart's plan was a modern mix of Neoclassical and Spanish Romanticism styles. Just as he had done at the Grove Park Inn, Grove hired masons from Italy for stone and tile work. Construction included reinforced concrete, wooden studs, and brick cladding.

George Durner was the son of one of the general contractors working on the hotel. Writer Rob Neufeld described Durner's recollection this way:

> "When the Battery Park Hotel and the Grove Arcade were being built," Durner recalled, "you had a number of black laborers that were digging ditches. They always would be singing a chant. If you were in my father's office with him on Haywood Street, you could hear this hum,

and all of a sudden it would stop, and when it did, he would run like mad to the job because he knew there (had been) an accident that had happened."

Accidents were more frequent than one would hope during construction, especially since workers blasted hills with dynamite. One blast was created with much more charge than was necessary and cracked the vestibule of the nearby St. Lawrence Church. Another blast killed Pomp Jenkins; a black laborer who was buried alive. Two steam shovel operators were also killed by an explosion. After these tragedies, Grove felt compelled to memorialize the workers who were killed, as well as the workers who labored on the project. Today, you can see this memorial above the ramps of the Grove Arcade, across the street from the Battery Park Hotel building. Icons represent an architect, a surveyor, a painter, a mason, a carpenter, and a steam shovel operator.

Completed in 1924, Grove's new Battery Park Hotel building stood fourteen stories tall and housed 220 rooms. Atop the hotel was a Mission Revival roof and dining area with incomparable views. Grove filled 17 train cars with furniture crafted in North Carolina to outfit the hotel.

Just as notable guests visited the original hotel, so too did celebrities visit the new one. When jazz musician Tommy Dorsey visited, he played in the hotel ballroom. Authors that visited included O. Henry, F. Scott Fitzgerald, and the ever-opinionated Thomas Wolfe.

When Wolfe visited the new hotel, as he did the original one, his response was quite different, as evidenced in his book, *You Can't Go Home Again*. Wolfe described the new Battery Park Hotel this way:

> "An army of men and shovels had advanced upon this beautiful green hill and had leveled it down to an ugly flat of clay, and had paved it with a desolate horror of white concrete, and had built stores and garages and office buildings and parking spaces--all raw and new--and were now putting up a new hotel beneath the very spot where the old one had stood. It was to be a structure of sixteen stories of steel and concrete and pressed brick. It was being stamped out of the same mold, as if by some gigantic biscuit-cutter of hotels that had produced a thousand others like it all over the country.

Just four years after opening it, Edwin Grove died at the Battery Park Hotel on January 27, 1927. Afterwards, others completed his vision for the Grove Arcade across the street.

Grove's hotel finally closed for business on October 30th, 1972. A bronze hotel register on Page Avenue downtown serves as the Battery

Park Hotel Urban Trail marker and lists the names of famous people that stayed at the original Battery Park hotel and at Grove's new Battery Park Hotel. The Battery Park Hotel building was placed on the National Register of Historic Places on July 14, 1977 and remains in the Downtown Asheville Historic District.

In 1979, Housing Projects, Inc. took over the building. Using preservation tax credits, the historic exterior remained intact. Now, the Battery Park Hotel building is owned by National Church Residences and is utilized as apartments for senior citizens, while the first floor houses business and retail stores.

On July 17, 1936, a murder occurred at the Battery Park Hotel that would be discussed for decades. Helen Clevenger was a 19-year-old New York University student visiting her uncle in Asheville at the Battery Park Hotel. Clevenger's body was found in Room 224 of the hotel. She had been shot in the chest, horrifically beaten, and her face slashed.

A hotel employee who had no history of violence was accused of the heinous crime and arrested. Martin Moore was a 22-year-old African-American who was developmentally disabled. Evidence presented for the case included a .32 caliber gun supposedly hidden in Moore's apartment. But this could have been planted. The grip of the gun had an unusual sharp point which prosecutors would claim had been used to cause the disfiguring injuries to the body.

Moore initially confessed to the crime, though later he recanted the confession and claimed that the police coerced him to confess. It has been suggested that the police only fingered Moore due to public pressure to make an arrest in the unsolved case. Moore's case went to trial in August of 1936. One eyewitness description of a suspect fleeing the scene did not match Moore's description. Despite this contradiction, and despite Moore recanting his confession, the jury deliberated only one hour before finding him guilty. The presiding judge declared the trial to be fair and Moore's motion to appeal was denied. Moore was executed in a gas chamber in Raleigh, North Carolina on December 11, 1936.

Residents at the Battery Park Senior Apartments report that strange occurrences are not uncommon and may be linked to Martin Moore or to Helen Clevenger. Some have experienced odd noises that cannot be explained. Others have heard angry voices that cannot be attributed to a living person in the vicinity. Still others report that, on stormy nights, Helen can be seen wandering the halls of the hotel.

One resident named Carol Hubbard gave her opinion on the matter: "I think Helen's ghost is here and I wouldn't be at all surprised if the man who was wrongly executed for her death is hanging around here, too."

Some suggest that early mornings are the best time to spot a ghost in the building. People working morning shifts have seen the spirit of an unidentified man in a pantry.

One woman I interviewed told me that, eight years prior, she worked in the Battery Park Hotel building when it housed a restaurant called Havana's. She told me that she had worked at the restaurant for about a year and a half when, one day, she was standing near the front entry. Suddenly, she heard a kitchen bell ring. Normally that is not an unexpected sound in the restaurant. The problem was, she knew that no one was in the kitchen at that moment. "It was very strange. It gives me chills to this day," she confided. "I've never experienced anything like that before. I worked there for many years after that and never experienced it again."

The male spirit reportedly witnessed in the building is possibly that of a government official named Clifton Alheit who committed suicide by jumping from the roof of the Battery Park Hotel on September 4th, 1943. Additionally, Alheit may not have been the only one to commit suicide at the site. According to some reports, people have seen the spectre of bodies falling from the roof.

After years of living across the U.S. and abroad, Lindsay H. currently lives in the Battery Park Senior Apartments. Though she has had experiences in the Battery Park building that she cannot explain, her otherworldly experiences began long ago.

"I lived in Colorado for 30-plus years," she told me. "For a number of years, I went to a church in Denver called the First Spiritual Science Church of Denver and psychic readings were done from the podium every Sunday. We were very active doing hands-on healings. I'm a Reiki Master myself and finished a lot of my Reiki studies there.

"The Spiritual Science churches do rescues to assist people, most often children, who are locked between this dimension and the other dimension. We were trained to how to do that. We would do a group meditation, pull the energy in, and then tell him or her that it was safe to move on, that there were spirits waiting for them on the other side.

"It was really quite interesting. But the spirits that had to be rescued were not in any way benevolent. They were panicked, frightened, uneasy. They would make their presence known and they would resist. They would fight us and we would hear banging. It was very difficult and unpleasant work. But we did it anyway. We would continue to work with specific entities until they were comfortable with leaving. They would indeed leave and go be free from being locked in this condition.

"I think that experience heightened my awareness. If you have a personal encounter with an entity that is terrified, usually young and frightened, not knowing what to do, you become more open to adult spirits that *are* more benevolent. It taught me the difference between torturous kinds of spirits and the spirits that just want to play and be acknowledged."

Lindsay's call to help others extended to animals, as well as spiritual entities.

"I worked in a wolf sanctuary in Denver," she told me. "We had 42 wolves and 82 cougars. It was broken up into different packs and fenced in. I was leaving very late one night. I typically didn't leave that late, but it was right around 9/11 and we were really struggling and trying to be supportive to each other. The animals were in chaos because they could pick up on our energy.

"I was driving home about 11:30 at night down the canyon. I saw a mountain lion on the side of the road and then suddenly my grandmother was sitting in the car next to me. I saw her body sitting there in the passenger seat! It was the same as if it was you sitting next to me in the passenger seat. It was totally unexpected. She was looking at the road and didn't say anything. I said, 'Grandma!' and as soon as the word came out of my mouth, she wasn't there anymore. She was gone.

"I had been thinking catastrophic thoughts about everything, thinking our country is coming to an end. Maybe that's why she appeared, to say, 'It's okay.' Because she always rescued me. My grandmother raised me until I was five. She always was my sanctuary for peace and comfort."

During Lindsay's first time living in Asheville, her experiences with the paranormal were more limited.

"I first came to Asheville in 2012," she explained. "I moved into The Meadows in West Asheville and was quite happy there. I never had any experiences there, other than an awareness when there were bears around when taking my dog, Abby, out at night. There were woods right near us and there were bears pretty frequently. I would get that sense. But never in the apartment. No experiences there."

After a few years working in the Caribbean, when it was time to settle into retirement, Lindsay chose Asheville once again.

"After being a corporate executive, I liquidated all my assets and then I retired. I moved back to Asheville from the Caribbean during July of 2019. I turned 70 and I thought, 'I don't know how long I'm going to be capable of being on the road.' My goal became going on the road with a built-out van, which I did. Before I left, I had applied to live at the Battery Park Senior Apartments. They had a three-year waiting list. I thought, 'Well, that'll be fine. In three years, I'll be able to assess it.' I was only on the road for eight months. It wasn't even a full year and then COVID hit. During that time, I was locked down in my van in a friend's driveway. Then Battery Park Apartments said, 'We have vacancies.' This was in 2020. I said, 'I thought it was three years?' They said, 'Many people have moved out because their family members want them closer to them.'

"I was offered an apartment on the fifth floor but my inner counsel told me that I don't want that apartment. I've learned to trust that. If my awareness is that 'This is not right, the energy isn't right,' then I don't even question it. They said, 'If you can wait a week or two, we'll have an apartment on the 10th floor and it is a corner.' I knew I wanted a corner. I wanted to have windows on both sides. I said, 'Waiting is not an issue. I've been living in my van for eight months. What's another two weeks?' After that, I moved in.

"In the apartment, I will periodically get what I would describe as a puff of air in my face. It's instantaneous and then it's gone. I'm very clear what that is. It's never near an open window. It's never outside. It's always in a completely still room, usually with no stimulus in the room: no television, no Twitter. Nothing like that. I'm a Buddhist and I meditate and read. But it's always benevolent."

Abby the dog also seems to sense when a spirit is present, in the apartment and throughout the building.

"When Abby was little, she barked all the time," said Lindsay. "I rented houses where we shared other levels with other people. I didn't want her to disturb them, so I would put my hand over her muzzle and she taught herself to bark with her mouth closed. Now, when there's people, she has an open mouth, full bark. But when something else is disturbing her, she does that low-level bark. A muffled sound of 'I'm not going to commit fully to this, but I want you to know that I don't like something. And I'm going to be quiet about it.' She does it sometimes with that puff of air in my face.

"I can't identify what that is. I just know that it doesn't frighten me. But it seems to be disturbing to her. I don't even say anything when it happens, but she gets up and starts wandering and pacing. That doesn't happen every time. If I have the puff of air while I'm in the living room and she's in the bedroom sleeping, she might miss it. But she's usually with me. She's usually within six feet of me all the time.

"I've come to learn for some time how clairvoyant my dog, Abby, is. She had a terrible time with the elevators, especially riding for ten stories. She really struggled for a couple of weeks, then she calmed down. I was sick during that first couple of months. All the new carpeting and drapes and furniture: all those chemicals. I discovered I had late-onset asthma. I had bronchitis for two months, so we didn't go out much. But after I got better, I began to realize that, with some regularity, she would get in the elevator with me and would stop as soon as her feet were in, then look up in the left-hand corner of the elevator. Then, she wouldn't move! She wouldn't go in any further. It was always the same corner, the same process. It was always and only in that corner. Even after she was inside the elevator, she would stare at that spot as the elevator moved for three or four floors. I was irritated by it, thinking it's still part of her reticence about the elevator. Until I realized, in my estimation, she was trying to alert me.

"When I began to realize this, I opened myself up more. I had been trained to acknowledge and experience these things through the church I used to go to in Denver. I then began noticing this in the same corner with a frequency. Not every day, but with regularity. I started acknowledging, 'OK, that's a benevolent spirit.'

"I began to get the belief and awareness that it was Zelda Fitzgerald. When this was a hotel, she and Scott Fitzgerald used to hang out here. She died just a few miles away, burned in a fire. I became so certain it was her that I began to talk to her as Zelda.

"In my experience with spirits, they will visit and visit and visit and drive you crazy until you acknowledge them. They just want to be acknowledged. Once you acknowledge them, they don't have that need to constantly be present or in some ways disturbing you. Because *they* know that *you* know. They don't need to justify their existence.

"Over time, this experience with Abby has decreased. Every once in a while, she'll do it. Same looking up to the ceiling, same staring at the same corner. I'll say, 'Zelda's with us,' and she relaxes. I relax. Then she doesn't pay any attention anymore. That's gone on for the better part of two years. But as the elevator experiences are decreasing the puff of air has been happening with greater frequency."

The elevator is not the only spooky area of the Battery Park Senior Apartments. Just ask Abby!

"There's a trash chute on each floor, in the north stairwell," Lindsay explained. "Something was going on there because Abby would not go in that stairwell with me! She would bark and bark. I would quickly throw the trash away while she waited out in the hall. I began to realize that it was not such a benevolent spirit.

"I picked up a book, which I haven't read yet, about a murder in this building. I have to say that I don't want to read the book because I don't want to anticipate that there's less than benevolent spirits. I know which apartment in the building the woman was killed in. But I don't walk around saying, 'Oh, do you have a ghost living in your apartment?' Nothing is really said about it."

Lindsay feels a connection with her neighbors that goes beyond sharing the physical space in the Battery Park building.

"There's an elder shaman guy who lives here. He said to me once, 'Oh, you live on the 10th floor. That's the spiritual part of the building. That section and up. The unawakened people live in the lower floors.' Which explains to me why I refused the fifth-floor apartment that was in better condition than the one I took. I just was so aware that I was not to be there. Of course, the views from the tenth floor are spectacular. But there's also more of a kindred spirit on these upper levels.

"He didn't call himself a shaman, because shamans don't call themselves shamans. He acknowledged Abby and he said, 'She's reading me.' I said, 'Yes, she is.' There are certain men in this building, and women, that she can't stand. She pulls away from them and withdraws.

"A couple of people on my floor have died. Whenever it happens, the police and EMTs would come. Abby and I ended up being on the elevator with a police officer. It took me everything I had to keep her from going after him. The officer said to me, 'We don't have good energy.' I said, 'How do you mean?' He said, 'We see and do things that dogs don't like. She's picking up on that.' Well, I was flabbergasted. I've dated police officers, but I've never known one that got that. He was very nice looking, very pleasant. But she did not want to be on that elevator with that guy. No, no, no, no, no, no, no, no. I thought that was fascinating. But I also believe that she's picking up on my energy and my reactions to things. I don't really like police officers that much. You don't be raised in Detroit and love police officers.

"Being born in Detroit, I also know to be aware. I am aware when there's dangerous people outside our building at night when I walk Abby. I am alerted by a spirit to be very vigilant about danger and watch all the way around me. I feel like that is a warning of safety that I'm being given. It never extends past the property. If I walk around the block, as soon as I get off the Battery Park property, then that protection presence leaves me and then I know I'm on my own. It stays with the building."

One of the most spectacular parts of the Battery Park building is the rooftop ballroom and garden area. The architecture is gorgeous and the view of the surrounding city and mountains is one of the best in Asheville. Apparently, it is as popular with the ghostly residents as with the living ones.

"We have a rooftop garden level on the top of the building, on 13th floor," Lindsay explained. "It was a ballroom and it's all glass. Usually, it's locked and I don't go up there very often. Not every time, but sometimes, as soon as the elevator door opens, it's filled with entities! It's different than the elevator persona. It's not Zelda. It's multiple people. We have a visiting nurse and when I go up there to see her, I'm totally aware that they're there. They're present and excited, joyous, happy that you're up there. They don't want anything from you. They just want to be acknowledged. It's like they're saying, 'Oh, don't go!' 'Thank you for visiting me,' is what I say. I never want to leave when I'm in there."

Lindsay's own spiritual journey has been one of learning and acceptance.

"When I still lived in the Caribbean, I got bladder cancer and had a very difficult time," she told me. "A relatively new friend of mine was a chanting Buddhist and they came to see me when I was in intensive care after a surgery. I said, 'I wish I could control this fear.' She said, 'I can tell you how you can control this fear. Let me teach you to chant.' She taught me and we chanted together. From that moment, I had no more fear around cancer. Zero. That kept me studying and going to her weekly meetings where we all chanted together for an hour and I learned the Japanese prayers for Nichiren Buddhism. From that point, I've been a practicing Buddhist. It does help me get very still and quiet and opens my capacity to be willing to accept and understand and appreciate things far greater than myself.

"Buddhism is not a religion, it's about philosophy. I am an ordained minister with a master's degree in Comparative Religion. I have married over 400 couples. In fact, I'm doing another wedding here on the 13th floor in a couple of weeks for a Jewish couple. She's writing her Jewish ceremony and I will deliver it. I don't judge. All paths lead to the divine in my thinking. Whatever works for you works for me.

"It's a matter of your level of willingness to embrace the notion that when we pass, we don't go anywhere. We're literally but a thought away. With the greater depth you believe that, with each one of those kinds of experiences, if you acknowledge it and you honor it, your ability to recognize it becomes greater. You get better at it and you don't feel frightened by it or alarmed in any way. It becomes comforting.

"When I'm in trouble, I call my father in. My father fought the Nazis in World War II in the Battle of the Bulge. I recently had an experience traveling in the van and I felt obliged to call him in. He immediately arrived and showed me that he had arrived by something that appeared in front of me. I know he's listening to this conversation and he's smiling about what he did. And I find that very comforting."

As part of being at peace with the world around her, Lindsay has come to terms with the spirits at the Battery Park building. And Abby is working on it.

"Is Zelda riding the elevator with us? I don't know," said Lindsay. "I don't feel alarmed anymore. In my mind, that amuses me, and so I assign that identity to it, and apparently it doesn't dislike that. I tell Abby it's just a garbage chute but she still doesn't want to go in the 10th-floor stairwell. But she's getting better at it."

THE BATTERY PARK SENIOR APARTMENTS ARE NOT OPEN TO THE PUBLIC. PLEASE BE RESPECTFUL OF CURRENT OCCUPANTS.

Battery Park Hotel and Hilltop

John Nolen Papers; 2903; Manuscripts; Division of Rare and Manuscript Collections, Cornell University Library; 9; https://rmc.library.cornell.edu/EAD/htmldocs/RMM02903.html, JSTOR, https://jstor.org/stable/community.545993. Accessed 10 May 2023.

Battery Park Hotel References

Blanton, Morgan. "A Haven in the Hills." *Cleveland County Schools*. Asheville Intensive. https://sites.google.com/a/clevelandcountyschools.org/asheville-intensive/battery-park-hotel. Web. Accessed March 4, 2020.

Calder, Thomas. "Asheville Archives: Flames finish off the original Battery Park Hotel, 1923." https://mountainx.com/news/asheville-archives-flames-finish-off-the-original-battery-park-hotel-1923/ Posted October 9, 2018. Web. Accessed 3/4/2020.

Calder, Thomas. "Life, death and drama in the Battery Park Apartments." *Mountain Xpress*. https://mountainx.com/news/life-death-and-drama-in-the-battery-park-apartments/ Posted on August 4, 2016. Web. Accessed March 4, 2020.

H., Lindsay. Interview with the author.

"Haunted Places along the Blue Ridge Parkway." *Virtual Blue Ridge*. https://www.virtualblueridge.com/articles/haunted-places/ Published July 6, 2013. Web. Accessed May 3, 2020.

Hunt, Max. "Horror in the highlands: Asheville's ghostly legends provide a glimpse into city's past." *Mountain Xpress*. https://mountainx.com/news/horror-in-the-highlands-ashevilles-ghostly-legends-provide-a-glimpse-into-citys-past/ Posted October 27, 2016. Web. Accessed May 8, 2020.

Neufeld, Rob. "Visiting Our Past: Asheville's history pivots on a hotel." *Citizen Times*. https://www.citizen-times.com/story/news/local/2017/07/23/visiting-our-past-ashevilles-history-pivots-hotel/497438001/. Published July 23, 2017. Updated July 24, 2017. Web. Accessed March 4, 2020.

Neufeld, Rob. "Visiting Our Past: Old Battery Park Hotel yielded to new in 1922". *Citizen Times*. https://www.citizen-times.com/story/news/local/2017/08/06/visiting-our-past-old-battery-park-hotel-yielded-new-1922/534827001/. Published August 6, 2017. Updated Aug. 7, 2017. Web. Accessed March 3, 2020.

sweis16. "Battery Park Hotel." https://www.wattpad.com/12135971-battery-park-hotel. Published February 11, 2013. Web. Accessed May 3, 2020.

Wikipedia contributors. "Battery Park Hotel." https://en.wikipedia.org/wiki/Battery_Park_Hotel. Web. *Wikipedia, The Free Encyclopedia*. November 7, 2018.

Wolfe, Thomas. (1940). *You Can't Go Home Again.* Harper & Row, 1940.

WEST ASHEVILLE

Asheville's reign as a tourism mecca began nearly 200 years ago in West Asheville. In February of 1827, Robert Henry became the earliest settler of West Asheville when he discovered a sulphur spring on his property there. Though the spring had the distinct odor of rotting eggs, it was a tremendous draw for its use as a beauty aid and perceived medicinal treatment for ailments such as arthritis and "dyspepsia."

By 1834, Henry and his son-in-law, Reuben Deaver, opened Deaver's Sulphur Springs, the first health resort in Asheville. It was a 250-room wooden hotel located 400 yards above the spring, in the area now known as Malvern Hills. The resort was renowned for entertainment including shuffleboard, billiards, bowling, horseback riding, and decadent French pastries. Live music in the ballroom enticed dancers beneath three chandeliers imported from Bavaria. Hotel business was booming until it burned down on March 13th, 1861.

In 1885, Edwin G. Carrier of Philadelphia purchased 1200 acres of land, including the sulphur spring. In 1887, Carrier opened the three-story Carrier's Springs hotel on the location of Deaver's previous hotel. Later called the Belmont, Carrier's hotel boasted a racetrack and the first electric passenger elevator in the South. Electrical service was provided to the area by the first electric power plant in Western North Carolina: a dam and powerhouse located nearby on Hominy Creek. Despite its brick construction, the Belmont, too, succumbed to fire in 1892.

In the late 1880s, the U.S. Post Office gave West Asheville its name. Situated southwest of downtown Asheville, West Asheville was originally considered part of Asheville, despite its location across the French Broad

River. But on February 9, 1889, West Asheville was incorporated as a separate town.

In 1891, to make it easier for Asheville tourists to travel to his Belmont Hotel, Carrier built the West Asheville and Sulphur Springs Electric Railway. The railway crossed the French Broad River on Amboy Road on what became known as "Carrier's Bridge."

For reasons lost to the sands of time, the incorporation charter for West Asheville was repealed on March 8, 1897, less than ten years after its inception. But that did not stop growth in the booming area. By 1910, tourists and locals could travel between Asheville and West Asheville by trolley. Streetcar lines ran west from downtown across the French Broad River, across the new West Asheville Bridge, and onward until the streetcar tracks ended near the intersection of Brevard and Haywood roads.

Haywood Road originated as Haywood Street in downtown Asheville, first passing the original Battery Park Hotel, crossing the French Broad River at Smith's Bridge, then climbing the hill to West Asheville through the area today known as Westwood. Haywood Road went on to follow the route of the Western Turnpike, which had crossed from Asheville to Haywood County since the 1850s. Now utilized as the principal route from downtown Asheville to the area west of the French Broad River, Haywood Road was the heart of West Asheville.

On March 13, 1913, the powers that be had yet another change of heart and West Asheville was incorporated for a second time. By 1914, H. L. Bright was elected the first mayor of West Asheville. He saw fit to pave Haywood Road to better serve the influx of people brought in by the trolley. The asphalt road was 60 feet wide and greater than a mile long. The town included ten stores, a bank, and a fire department to serve its 4,000 residents.

In what was becoming a bad habit, the mayors of both Asheville and West Asheville proposed to rejoin the two towns as one in order to handle growing municipal debt and pressures for expansion and improvement. In the first election in Western North Carolina to use a secret ballot, support for the merger of the towns passed by only eight votes. The annexation occurred on June 9, 1917 and West Asheville's then 6,000 residents bumped up Asheville's total population to 30,000.

By 1916, construction had begun on the earliest buildings located at the intersection of Brevard and Haywood roads, an area growing due to its location as the turnaround point at the end of the streetcar line. Most were two-story brick buildings intended for commercial use.

The streetcar trolleys ran on Haywood Road until 1934, when service to West Asheville ceased. The 700 and 800 blocks of Haywood Road are now known as the West Asheville End of Car Line Historic District. Many of the buildings there have been lovingly restored and are the heart of one of Asheville's most popular neighborhoods.

The first structure built at 732 Haywood Road dates back to the 1910s and housed a grocery store. During the 1920s, the OK Lunch Room and Dowtin's Bakery operated at the location but they were replaced in the 1930s by Atkins Service Station. In the 1940s, the Standard Lunch operated there but was closed by the county in 1948 "to drive booze and gambling from the city," according to the *Asheville Citizen-Times*. In 1954, the vacant storefront re-opened as Bon Ton Cleaners followed by several restaurants. The building currently houses a clothing store and a guitar shop.

The Franklin Building at 751 Haywood Road was built in 1923. Its tenants have included Sterchi Brothers men's store through the 1930s, several grocery stores, a drug store, and the Home Furniture Company through 1945. May's Market, which operated in the adjacent building originally, expanded into the Franklin Building in 1950 and the business flourished there until 1978. Today, the building houses Nine Mile, a Caribbean fusion restaurant that is a favorite of this author.

In 1929, the West Asheville Post Office moved into to new digs at 795 Haywood Road, a two-story brick structure dating back to 1912. The post office remained in this building through 1965, when it moved to a nearby location on Patton Avenue. In recent years, 795 Haywood Road has been home to the Wright Creative photography company.

The Art Deco style Isis Theater was built at 743 Haywood Road for a cost of $50,000. It opened as a single-screen movie theater on December 26, 1937 and charged 20 cents for an adult ticket. The theater operated only until November of 1957. During the next decades, it went through a series of closures and remodels. Until recently, it operated as the Isis Music Hall, which featured outdoor events, a restaurant, and a stage for musical acts.

During the height of commercial development along Haywood Road in West Asheville during the late 1920s, several properties were built by James T. Bledsoe, owner of J.T. Bledsoe & Company, a real estate and insurance firm. In 1928, Bledsoe built the Palace Theater building at 791 Haywood Road which operated until the mid-twentieth century. It is currently the bodega La Catrachita Tienda Hispana. In 1929, Bledsoe built a two-story brick building at 797 Haywood Road whose initial tenant was the Great A&P Tea Company who operated a grocery there. It currently houses the Alley Cat Social Club.

James Bledsoe made his most indelible mark on West Asheville in 1927 when he constructed the Bledsoe Building at 775 Haywood Road for $65,000 and carved his name into the very facade. It is the largest building on Haywood Road. The unique brick structure is trapezoid-shaped and has two stories and two-tiered porches on the rear side. Originally, the first floor was comprised of eight retail spaces while the top floor was divided into residential rentals. Sadly, four short years after completing the building, Bledsoe defaulted on the property loan. On August 31, 1931, the property was sold at auction to an investor in Virginia for $45,000. Between 1931 and 2014, the property changed hands only four times, including to the current owner.

Despite many renovations through the years, the Bledsoe Building still retains much original woodwork, tin ceilings, screen doors, two-panel doors with transoms, and its original Craftsman style staircase. Through the years, the historic West Asheville landmark has been home to plumbers, groceries, bakeries, cafes, pharmacists, realty offices, furniture stores, and dentists. Current tenants include a brewery and restaurant, a natural foods market, a video store, and a salon. The western side of the building displays one of West Asheville's most recognized murals: a painting of Dolly Parton and RuPaul that was featured on the show "RuPaul's Drag Race."

A dear family friend pointed me to a West Asheville couple who have some amazing tales to tell about their lives. From their time growing up with their families in West Asheville until they met each other and eventually married, Tonya and Jamie have had extraordinary experiences, both individually and together. I first spoke with Tonya, who was born in Asheville.

"I was born in Mission Hospital," Tonya began. "I grew up in a trailer park in the Skyland area but I have a lot of family in Spruce Pine. We're a pretty close family and I used to stay up there a lot. My cousins and I were up there playing hide and seek at night. There were three pioneer guys sitting there with the old school pioneer hats and beards! They turned around and smiled at us. It scared us and we went screaming. Only one of my cousins will admit that she remembers this. It was a really religious family, so it was frowned upon to talk about that stuff.

"About 1983, when I was seven, my stepfather bought a house on Brownwood Avenue in West Asheville to be closer to his mother. I could literally do the whole Red Riding Hood thing and go through the woods to get to my grandmother's house. He got a really good deal on the house but it wasn't built very well. It had a lot of work that needed to be done. Like the carpets were tacked to the floor. Snow would blow in through the walls. We only had a wood stove. It was definitely making ends meet just to survive.

"My room was really drafty, really cold, and weird-feeling sometimes. My friends told me that, before we moved in, a very poor family lived there. They said that the little girl that stayed in my room had gotten sick and passed away there. I would hear my name all the time. It sounded like a kid calling my name. Like, 'Tonya!' I'd ask Mom, 'Did you call me?' And she'd say, 'No.' But I heard somebody say my name specifically.

"There was one time I remember seeing a lady. The door to my room was open and she came in. She had light hair. I couldn't see her face very well, or details, but her dress was interesting. It was very long and tapered at the waist. She waved at me and left! It wasn't bad. It was just weird. And it was scary, as a kid.

"I wasn't able to have people come and stay with me until we got the house fixed up a little bit better. That's when I got more confirmation that I wasn't the only one seeing things. I wouldn't say anything to anybody. I didn't want to scare them. But, my best friend, she was so scared. They're like, 'I just saw this,' or 'I just heard this,' or 'I felt something touch me.' I'm like, 'Okay, I'll watch your back. You watch my back. If we see anything, we'll be okay.' Stuff would go missing, like toys. Sometimes it was my favorite toys! I'd be like, "Where did they go?" And then they would show back up.

"I would hear knocking up near the ceiling, but coming from the outside of the house. You could hear it start from one end of the house and go all the way down. It was like, Knock! Knock! Then further down, Knock! Knock! The ceiling was really high. I don't know how anybody could reach that high. There's no way. They'd have to be on a ladder and there's no ladder up there. And this happened all the time.

"My boyfriend, Jamie, now my husband, we've been together for a very long time. Since we were kids."

Tonya explained that Jamie experienced odd things in her house, too. I spoke to him about his experiences.

"There was something we saw one night just for a second," Jamie told me. "It was at the upper corner of the living room in her parents' house. It looked like a weird elf creature. We heard knocking and scratching all night. Tonya's like, 'You need to go home.' I was like, 'I won't leave you alone with this shit!' She was like, 'It's fine. Don't worry about it. It happens all the time.' Right when we're talking about it, there was more knocking on the house. I ran outside, but there was nothing there."

"The house was built really weird," Tonya explained. "Like a really long tunnel in the middle and then the bedrooms went off to the side. If I had to get up to go pee in the night, I swear, in that hallway I would see these things that looked like people all dressed differently. Some had pretty dresses on. But it's like they weren't walking. I don't know how to explain it. They were drifting in a line, but like they didn't know where they were going. I don't know where they were going or what they were doing, but I could easily see it. I don't think they were trapped there. I think they were lost or looking for something, looking where to go. It was almost like, people going to a train station. Like a transient place.

"If I would bring anything up, my mom would say, 'We don't talk about stuff like that.' So, I wonder if she saw stuff too and was afraid to say anything.

"The creepiest spot was our laundry room, which was the first room when you come in the door. It was always so cold in there. Even after it got insulated, it was just really cold. I started feeling different things coming around.

"When my older brother moved out, I got to move into the bigger bedroom. Then my little brother got my room. My little brother would mention stuff to me every once in a while. You could feel things watching you. I had one friend who stayed the night. She stayed in what was my old bedroom. I hadn't told her anything. I go in there to say, 'Hey, good morning!' and she had the covers up to her face. She was like, 'Your house is not okay.' I was like, 'Oh. You felt it, didn't you?' She's like, 'There's something going on here. I don't know if I want to come back.'

"I did have a lot of dream activity. I actually started getting confused of whether I was awake or asleep. I used to have a lot of dreams come true with that house, too. Sometimes it was simple stuff, dumb stuff, everyday things. Like, one day I told my friend, 'Hey, so-and-so is going to say this to you in the lunch line. You might want to have a good comeback for it.' And it happened. She's like, 'What?! This really happened!' I was like, 'Yeah, I have dreams like this all the time.'

"We all had a favorite janitor named Oliver that used to work at Hall Fletcher. It was sixth and seventh grade then. Everybody liked him. I had a dream that he was dead. I saw the police and I saw the house. I walked in that morning and was like, 'Has anybody seen Oliver today? I had this dream.' He didn't show up. He had been killed that night.

"I do feel that I had a strong connection with 'the other side.' It scared me really bad and I tried to push a lot of it away. What do you do with it? You start feeling like, 'I'm going crazy.' But I still have those dreams every once in a while."

"I had a bad Ouija board experience there. We were in sixth grade at the time and a group of friends was at my house, some I knew better than others. One of my friends was like, 'Let's play with a Ouija board!' I was like, 'I don't want to use it.' But my best friend, she was participating. We were burning candles and that kind of stuff. They asked it a question and it spelled out, 'Robert is dead.' Then, right after that, my best friend's phone rang. Her cousin was two years old and his name was Robert. It was her mom calling to say that Robert had passed away. I was like, 'No. This thing is gone, out of the house.' I don't think Ouija boards are good things.

"There was just so much stuff going on at that house, good and not so good. Eventually, I felt better about the Brownwood Avenue house because I was doing cleanses. I feel like it helped a lot with the creepy feelings and negative stuff going on there. My parents had no idea I was doing it. I kept everything to myself after I found out they weren't really open to me talking about it. I kept a lot of stuff hidden.

"About 1995, after I turned 17, I moved out. I was super happy about moving out. That house is still there, though. And I still have dreams about that house."

Tonya believes that the oddities of the Brownwood house were partly due to the area where it was located.

"This stuff happens a lot in these older neighborhoods," she suggested. "It's the whole area over there, near Brownwood. I've had friends that lived over there and they experienced stuff as a kid, too. My husband would stay at some friends' houses that were near the Brownwood house and they had a lot of weird stuff going on."

While living in the Brownwood Avenue house as a child, Tonya admired a home on nearby Dorchester Avenue, which runs between Haywood Road and Patton Avenue.

"There was a house on Dorchester I always infatuated with," she told me. "It was fairy-tale like. Such a cool house. And big, too. Really big! I remember going there with my mom when I was a kid to pick up typesetting because my family had a printing company. At that time, typesetting was done in a different place than the printing. We'd go to that house to pick up stuff from the basement.

"Jamie's mom's friend owned that house. She had moved away and wanted somebody to keep it up. So, we moved into it! It was such a storybook house. When we first moved in, it felt magical. The back yard was cool. There's a pond and nature. Really serene. I couldn't believe I was there.

"But it had a weird basement. Bizarre! There were a whole bunch of fire extinguishers in the basement when we moved in. And a whole bunch of old school chairs down there. I'm not sure why. I do feel like that house has a lot of history to it.

"When we moved in, Jamie had his own room. His mom had her own room and his brother and his family also had a room. I had my own room. It was a really big place! My bedroom had its own little entrance and bathroom. There was this huge living room that goes up to another tiny area. Every time I was in that tiny area, I swear, I felt like there were people playing cards. Like a group of grouchy old men playing cards and smoking. I don't feel like they were interested in me at all.

"Jamie was definitely experiencing stuff there, too. Sometimes it would be goofy stuff. I'm gonna be straight up honest. We would see weird lights in the sky at the Dorchester house. I can't explain it. One time we saw this weird blue thing come from the sky through the window and it hit Jamie right in the eye! I saw it and I was like, "What was that?" His mom was doing her makeup and she didn't see anything. I don't know where it came from. I don't even know how to explain anything like that.

"There, and at the Brownwood house, I would have weird dreams that I was getting sucked out of a window. In the dream, I'm trying to scream and get help, but I never really saw what was going on. I just knew something was wanting to get me out the window. I've actually felt like that since I was four years old.

"After two or three years, the owner ended up passing away and we had to move out of that house. I was sad because it was a really nice place. I felt like anything that was there was not bad at all. Like it was people doing activities that they used to do, even though they might not be there physically anymore."

Jamie, hasn't just had brushes with the dead. He has been dead himself.

"I've actually died a couple of times," Jamie told me. "I was born dead. I had the cord around my neck and I wasn't breathing. I was purple. They didn't expect that because apparently that wasn't how it was in the womb. I got twisted up somehow. It's probably my fault. I wouldn't be surprised.

"I have an insane a memory of everything that's happened to me. I remember my mom feeding me and I remember learning how to walk. I've always wanted to fly since I was a baby, since I can remember. In the late '70s, we lived in Livingston Heights, which was the projects. I was walking with my mom and she was talking to a friend of hers. As we were walking, I realized that I was floating. I remember I felt like I was flying. I looked down and saw my body sitting on the sidewalk, propped up against a fire hydrant. I felt like I was hanging over them, leaning forward over them in a weird way. I tried to get my mom's attention but she wouldn't pay any attention to me. But then she started looking weird, like she could see me for a second. Then I snapped back into my body. Right then, she turned around and said, 'Were you saying something to me?' And I was like, 'Yeah, I was trying to get your attention! I was flying over you!' I don't know if I died again or what the hell happened."

"I've seen ball lightning a couple of times when I was a kid," Jamie told me. "I saw it twice and both times it came at us, like it was alive. One time, when I was a really little kid, it was burning the side of my uncle's house. We went out and he got a stick and was going to poke it. I was like, 'Don't poke that with a stick!' But when he would get near it, it would move away. Then, as soon as he moved away, it would come at him! Then, there was an audible, really loud 'POP!' and it was gone. It happened again at another house where he lived in New Mexico. We walked out to see it and it was coming at us. We're backing away and it was moving around bushes to come close to us. That time it made these weird cracking noises. Then it fizzled out and was just gone. You could smell it, like burning rubber. That was a trip! Really strange."

As a kid, Jamie's experiences with the unusual were not limited to the paranormal. One very real event in particular terrified him.

"We lived in a place in Montford, which was formerly a very rich part of town, but during the '70s, became a bad part of town. I was so poor growing up that it was still very nice to me. These huge, grand, old houses that were built at the turn of the century, you could get them cheap because nobody wanted to live in the neighborhood. In the early '80s, we lived in one on Elizabeth Place. We lived in that house with a lot of people: my mom, my aunt, and her two daughters who both had younger kids.

"At that house, I was in the fifth grade. Every night, I was reading *It*, which is an absolutely terrifying book. So, I'm scared to death. Like, terrified! My mom was just like, 'You're doing so good, reading that giant book.' And I'm like, 'It's scaring me.' She goes, 'Does it scare you bad enough not to read it?' 'No.' 'Well, finish reading the book.' I'm like, 'You don't understand how scary this thing is.'

"We came home one day. I was sitting on the bed and I was hearing this thumping noise. I thought it was the family downstairs, because we'd all come home at once. Then, I felt something thump the bed. I was like, 'I think there's something under the bed.' So, I lean over the edge and I looked down. There was a guy under my bed! He slides out on his back, smiling at me, a huge smile. I start screaming and I jump up. I started running down the stairs to go where my mom and everybody was. The guy jumps all the way down this huge flight of stairs and runs out the door in front of me.

"This guy could run really fast. My dad was an amazingly fast runner and he ran at least as fast as him. Luckily, my mom actually saw him, or nobody would have believed me. We don't know what he was doing, if he just picked that place to hide or if he was after me.

"After that, I slept with a giant knife. My mom let me do it. She was like, 'It's fine. I'll knock on the door before I come in and I won't surprise you.' Everybody agreed: nobody go in my room unless you knock on the door and I answer you. That's what we did for months and months. It took me almost a year to stop sleeping with the knife.

"That was nice and terrifying. Nightmare stuff! I can still see him. I still see the look in his eyes and his giant smile. That's never going to go anywhere. I could pick him out of a lineup if I saw this guy. They never got him because we lived in a poor part of town and it's like, 'Oh, it's just some poor people getting harassed by another poor person.' That was another rattling experience that I didn't really need."

"That house was the first time I realized that something's going on that I can't see and I don't know what it is. Something's going on that I don't know anything about. In that house, I would hear talking and noises like somebody coming in and out of the house. Like somebody coming home. At first, I always thought it was the family. But later, when I knew damn well I was by myself, I started hearing cabinets open and close and furniture getting scooted. Or my mom would be in her room and I'd hear all this stuff downstairs. I'd come downstairs and then hear it in the next room. But I'd walk in there and there would be nothing. It would be dead silent.

"Then, I started hearing people talking in the hallway in the middle of the night. I'd hear a man outside my door. Like a grown man voice. And there were no men that lived in this house! I knew about ghosts from movies, so it was the first thing I thought, of course. I'd be so scared. I would put stuff against my door sometimes.

"I didn't say anything because I didn't think anybody would believe me. My family and I, we will make an immense amount of fun of each other. The more I love you, the more garbage you're going to hear about yourself from me. That's just how I grew up. It's out of love but that's what we do. So, I didn't want to make a big deal about it. I kept to myself a lot. Then my cousin Connie started saying, 'You hear somebody in the hallway, right?' And I was like, 'Well, I hear all of y'all.' And she goes, 'No, you hear a man speaking, don't you? I heard it talking. Then it sounds like somebody was rearranging furniture downstairs.'

"I had never brought that up. I'd never said one thing about that. I was like, 'Yeah, like in the kitchen.' She goes, 'Yeah, like scooting chairs. I thought that was you at night, messing around.' I was like, 'No, that is not me. I don't know what the hell that is. It sounds like something scooting chairs and thumping around and going through the cabinets.' So, we agreed on that. It was the first person that corroborated anything I'd heard because I had never brought it up. Connie was a very, very tough chick and I really looked up to her as a child. To hear her say that meant a lot to me.

"We didn't live there much longer after that. We got a nicer place, which was actually a step down because those old houses are amazing. I wish we could've stayed there, even with a ghost. Maybe not the guy under the bed. That's not good. But it was a beautiful house and you could never afford it now, because that part of town is way too expensive to live in."

Jamie's bizarre life experiences were fated to continue even after leaving the Montford house and its creepy smiling man under the bed. He and his family moved but remained in the Asheville area.

"We came back to West Asheville, to Brevard Road," he told me. "I was in the sixth grade. We had a couple of boarders that my mom was letting stay there for money. They were up all the time, day and night, just being weird as hell. I did have a really horrific experience there.

"We didn't have a VCR but I was getting into horror movies. My mom worked with a girl who had two kids, a brother and a sister. They hadn't been here in Asheville very long and didn't have any friends. Even though they were older than I was, like junior high school, they kind of dumped us together. I never met these guys before, ever. We were watching that movie, *C.H.U.D.* It gets to the Daniel Stern part where they're showing all the containment hardware, boots, a containment suit, and stuff. I'm into this movie. Like, super absorbed. Then, I hear the girl start screaming. She's screaming like she's getting murdered. Because she *was* getting murdered. I turn around and the guy has a knife and he's attacking her. He's stabbing his own sister in the head. She's got her arms up and he's stabbing through her hands and stabbing her arms. I jump up and start punching him as much as I can. He turned around with the knife at me and I backed up a little bit. When he turned back to her, I got on him again and started punching him more. I start screaming at him as loud as I can and he runs and locks himself in the bathroom.

"I asked the girl, 'What the hell's going on?' She's like, 'I don't know. He's never done this before.' I called my mom at work and she calls the cops from there. She's like, 'Get a weapon for if he comes out.' I got a meat tenderizing hammer and a knife. The girl is bleeding everywhere and freaking out. I told her, 'If he comes out, I'm going to kill this guy.'

"The cops and paramedics come. They're talking to him through the door but he won't open it, so they kick it in. He has cut himself to ribbons. I'll never forget what he looked like when they got him out. His blood is everywhere. And I had to clean the bathroom!

"They moved. They were gone within like days of that. I never heard anything about why this happened or if he was okay or if she was okay. To this day, I wonder what happened. And it messed up *C.H.U.D.* for me. I couldn't finish that movie for another ten years because that's all I could think about. I'm such a cinephile and I was like, 'I want to finish *C.H.U.D.*, but I don't want to have the nightmares again.' When *Home Alone* came out with Daniel Stern, I was like, 'I'm never watching *Home Alone*.'

Jamie's spooky experiences began again while living in West Asheville.

"I lived in a place that we called 'The Alamo' because it looked like The Alamo. My mom got it really cheap because it used to be a storefront. It was a terrible little place. There was almost no insulation. It's on a blind curve where everybody would haul ass around. You'd always think someone's going to crash through the house.

"I was throwing myself into music with my friends and realized that I could write songs. That was when Tonya and I first started seeing each other. Tonya used to come over all the time. We were just friends for a while, which was stupid. After you realize you love somebody, you're like, 'Why weren't we dating a long time ago?' But I guess that's just how that goes.

"That house was another creepy spot, especially down in the basement. Mom was like, 'You can do whatever in the basement. I don't care if you knock holes in the wall, you can graffiti the place. I don't care. Just stay out of trouble when you're not here.' So, we hung out a lot there. It was a couple of little rooms and one hallway. I'd go down there to play my bass at night and every time I would hear shuffling, like feet in the hallway. But there would be nobody there. I'm trying to play this bass, but every time, I'm stopping! I was like, 'You're bugging me, man! If you're gonna come out, come out. I'm tired of doing this.' After a while, I just stopped giving it attention.

"Around 1990, we moved from that place to the Wake Robin house in Oteen. It was right off the interstate. I guess they bought that property and thought, 'Well, I can't build shit here because there's so much mountain. So, I'm just going to dig into the mountain and put a house here.' You could see they'd dug away and leveled that. That was right outside the back door. It always felt really intimidating. It felt like the house shouldn't be there.

"Apparently nobody had lived in this house for a very long time, since the '70s. There was a den downstairs with a bar and one of those fireplaces with a hood over it. The carpet was green and yellow shag all through this house. Everything about it felt old. The air was old. There were cool '70s chairs I wanted to keep. But when we moved in, they had thrown out all the furniture and broke it.

"The house was in a really quiet part of the neighborhood. By that time, I had hair to my ass, so I definitely was frowned on. Everybody looks at you like you shouldn't be there.

"The driveway was really, really steep. Like stupidly steep. People used to trip and fall down that damn thing when they'd come over, every time. And it's hard to drive your car up there without bottoming out. A lot of people wouldn't come over because there's nowhere to park. My mom worked all the time and I was 15 and I couldn't get my permit yet to drive. So, I was out there in this big house all by myself. I was lonely as I could possibly be out there.

"The first couple of days we were there, I started having these dreams about a little boy who kept coming into my room. He had a bowl haircut, little shorts, and a little blue shirt. He looked like a '70s kid to me 'cause I dressed like that then. He looked like somebody I would have hung out with when I was a kid.

"He would come in my room and I would just be like, 'Get out! I don't even know who you are.' Then I would realize that I was awake, sitting up on the bed, yelling. I don't know if I had dreamed enough to get upset and wake up to do that, or if I was already awake and yelling at something. I have no idea. That was the first two days I was there! I think because I was so freaked out by it, that's why I had the dream again. Or at least, that's what I was telling myself.

"This is the most ridiculous thing ever: you'd be in the kitchen making a sandwich. Say you pop the top off the peanut butter. You'd put the lid on the counter and you turn around. When you turn back, the lid would be gone! I could put a fork down: it would be gone. Or it would be moved. No sound. Absolutely no sound at all. This went on to where I was having to plastic wrap jars because I couldn't find any lids. My mom was like, 'What are you doing with lids?' I'm like, 'I'm not doing this.' She was like, 'I know you're having a hard time out here.' I'm like, 'No, that is not the point. I don't even know how to describe this to you, but stuff disappears when you turn around.' Then later, you'd open the refrigerator and the lids would be in there. Or sometimes they'd be on the floor or in an entirely different room. Forks and spoons would be laying on the counter all weird, or in weird places. I'd think, 'I was just here and there was nothing here!' And me being by myself so much, I *know* that nobody else did that.

"One time we're sitting watching TV on the couch and I saw what looked like the beach ball monster from that John Carpenter movie, *Dark Star*. It jumps up and down. I saw that at the corner of my eye. I looked at my mom and she started looking in that direction. She looked back at me and I was like, 'You saw something, didn't you?' She's like, 'I didn't see anything.' I was like, 'I know you're totally lying to me.' She wouldn't admit it. That's the only time that she saw something weird that I *know* she saw.

"I used to get random shocks all the time there. Also, there was a giant, weird, handprint-looking thing in the carpet in the bathroom. When you were in that shower, it always looked like someone was in the bathroom with you, walking around. A shadow with a lumbering gait like Bigfoot. It would walk past you while you're washing your hair. I never saw anything else in that bathroom unless I was in the shower, only when

I was in the shower. But, then, I would see stuff all the time, like incessantly. Like three times per shower.

"Also, I would wake up in the other room, a storage room beside my bedroom. I'd wake up lying on the floor in my underwear and be absolutely freezing and not remember getting up and going in there.

"Then, I started hearing all these noises. It sounded like a little kid. When mom was at work, I'd be in my room, but I'd hear noises like somebody was walking up and down the stairs. Or I would walk up and down the stairs and, I swear, it sounds like somebody was walking behind me on the stairs.

"My friends were a year or two younger than me, so they couldn't drive. But every once in a while, they would come out and see me and hang out. We'd try to jam or something. One time when they were there, I started walking down the stairs and about halfway down, I'm hearing it behind me. They all look at me like, 'What in the hell?' I stop quick, but it goes BUMP BUMP down two more steps, like it didn't stop fast enough. I was like, 'Okay, we all heard that. That was not a joke.' I finished walking downstairs and there was no noise. I get to the bottom of the stairs and I turn around. It goes, BUMP BUMP BUMP BUMP BUMP BUMP BUMP down the stairs to right where I am, like playing catch up. I almost shit myself! I was like, 'Oh my God! Why did I do that?'

"That became a game for us. You could jump a stair, jump another stair, and it would do the same thing right after you. It was like almost like we were speaking to this thing. In my head, I knew it was this kid. I knew it.

"One time, when Andrew Dice Clay had just come out with a tape, a friend thought this would be funny to listen to. I was like, 'This sounds like relatives of mine.' While we were listening from the next room, we heard this loud THUMP and the tape stopped. I was like, 'I bet that kid wrecked your player.' We go look and there was a broken drumstick stabbed all the way through this huge piece of cardboard. The tape player was open and the tape was on the floor. I was like, 'The kid doesn't like this, man.'

"I had this weird dream one night where the kid came in the room. Then I realized that I was awake. I'm sitting there and I couldn't really see it. It was like an outline of a kid. It hit me and I said, 'Are you lonely? Are you okay?' It didn't speak words. I didn't hear a voice, but something told me that this is all happening because the house is cut into the hill. It let something out. The kid is there, but whatever this other thing is, it is let out because the house is where it's not supposed to be. It shouldn't be there. That it was wrong when they cut into the hill. And that's what I felt the day I saw that house! It freaked me the hell out.

"So much creepy stuff was happening up there that was scaring me, I moved from my room upstairs down into the den. Once I moved down there, none of that stuff ever happened. Down there, I always felt like some older man was mad at me and I wasn't supposed to be in there. It reminded me of my dad. But nothing ever happened down in that room.

"When we moved out, I could feel the sadness in the air. I could really feel genuine 'somebody-had-died feelings' when we left that house. All I could think of was that little kid. He was lonely and trying to hang out with us by playing on the stairs and messing with the lids. I kept having this feeling like I just lost a relative.

"It feels like it's an entity that is aware. That's what always weirds me out. It's not something just repeating itself. It is something that has a brain and it's thinking, or at least it's aware of me, too. Something going, 'Hey, you!' where I'm going, 'Ahhhh, get away from me!' Which is your natural instinct. But then, after years, it was like, 'Maybe don't get away...' But the other things that were going on was because the house didn't belong there.

"We only lived there for a little over a year but Tonya and I kept talking about it. Later, she was like, 'I want to see that house.' So, we go out there. When we drove up, I pointed out my room. Tonya grabs my arm and starts freaking out. You could see the shadow-shape of the little boy standing in the window, looking out. Tonya lost it and I lost it. I felt that same immense, horrible sadness, like I'd abandoned him. Which is really a weird feeling. I know what happened now. This kid was just looking for some connection. It totally broke my heart and I still feel sad about it."

Both Jamie and Tonya can attest to the fact that the Bledsoe Building is haunted. They have lived and worked in that building in the very heart of West Asheville, spending a great deal of time there. They related to me some hair-raising experiences they've had there.

"That is an extremely old building," Jamie said of the Bledsoe Building. "You had a trolley system and there was a turnaround here for the trolleys because this was the end of Asheville. We were going to get one of the first subways in America because Asheville was a hell of a boomtown but the depression just crushed us. We have really rare Art Deco buildings downtown that were built during that time. There's tunnels all under Asheville and West Asheville, too, where they built them and then just abandoned them. My dad was a cop here during the '60s. He said that one time he had been down in one of the tunnels. There was a big hole in a wall downtown. When he got under there, there was a huge, cavernous railway-looking system with no tracks that was full of homeless people living there. He was like, 'I had no idea this existed.'"

Jamie and Tonya lived in an apartment in the upstairs of the Bledsoe Building.

"We lived in an apartment upstairs above the Westville Pub," Tonya told me. "This was years ago, before the new owners bought it. We would see interesting stuff up there every once in a while."

"That apartment was a weird place. Tonya started sleepwalking a lot," Jamie explained. "Where you go in to the building, it's pretty steep stairs to the apartment above. One time, as I'm walking up the stairs, on the landing I see a guy with a giant hat and giant, square shoulders. I immediately knew what that was. It was definitely a zoot suit. I'm watching him and he's putting a cigarette to his mouth and lighting it. I couldn't really see features but I've seen a million people light a cigarette, so I knew what was happening. It hits me that he's yellow all over. The whole thing was a yellowish color: the outfit and himself, his hands, and the side of his face. I wouldn't say glowing. A really dull look to the entire thing. Then, just when I got high enough on the stairs to see it better, it walked across the hallway towards my apartment and then walked into the wall, right into where our apartment is.

"I went, 'Holy shit!' I almost dropped everything I had. I went in the apartment and asked Tonya, 'Did you see that?' But she didn't. I completely flipped the hell out. I started looking around and saw that where he had walked into that wall is actually sealed off. You could see that wall had been patched up where a door used to be there at some point. So maybe it's some kind of repetitive thing. But I never saw that again."

On the first floor of the Bledsoe Building, Jamie was employed at Orbit DVD.

"I've been working at Orbit for almost 16 years," he told me. "It's a great place. We have a huge paranormal section. It used to be just DVDs but it's changed a lot. The entire back room used to be all rentals. It was full of huge shelves that you couldn't see over, so it was a little labyrinthine.

"At night, you cut off the lights and it's a straight shot to walk out the door. You don't walk very far to get out of there once you turn lights off. There's not many lights and one window that would be to my left. To my right, out of the corner of my eye, I would see my shadow walking. For a while, I thought it was a weird reflection of some sort. But then it started to hit me, it looked like it was a little off time. I would joke about it and then I wouldn't see anything for a month or two, then I would see it again. I thought, 'That's weird that it's not consistent' because the light in here is always consistent. It doesn't change. One time, as a joke to myself, I was walking and I stopped. The shadow kept walking. This was at the end of a pretty long aisle and I could distinctly see the legs moving. It kept walking until I couldn't see it.

"It freaked me out, but I was like, 'That was probably my imagination.' I walked through the place in the dark, looking, but I don't see anybody. Nobody's hiding or running away because there's nowhere to go. I would see that at least every couple of weeks.

"Another time, I was about to walk down an aisle. When we used to rent, we had these slips you had to put back in the cases. I was like, 'I have to put these damn things up or I'm gonna hear about it in the morning.' I go down this dark aisle but I know where everything is because I do this all the time. I look up and it was a shadow standing there. I could clearly see the outline. It was almost like somebody wearing a hoodie. It was completely dark and I couldn't see through this thing. What I see is this gunfighter pose: legs spread out, arms down, kind of hunched like a gunfighter. Or like an 'I'm getting ready to run' pose. It's at the end of the aisle standing like that.

"I'm not a scaredy cat when it comes to people. I've been in a million fights and I've punched a lot of assholes. When I saw it standing there, I automatically think somebody is in the store and they're going to get me. Well, I'm not going to get attacked by somebody while I'm working here. So, I pulled out my knife and I run at it. It turns to the right and runs off in the same direction it always goes. There's absolutely nowhere to go in that corner. And I ran at it and then it was gone! When I got to that end,

I felt a very cold breeze coming through there. And this is the middle of the summer.

"I turned around just left. Got out of there. I didn't see it again for months and months. But then it would do the same thing. Every month, I would see a leg going behind a shelf, like when somebody's walking and you just see the last part of the leg going behind something. That's what I saw, but just when the lights were off. And that's the weirdest thing because it was a shadow creature in the dark. At that time, you could see through the windows, so you could see out. There was more light coming from behind it than coming from my way, but I could not see through the thing in front of a painted window. It's crazy to me that it's still blocking light somehow. That's why I thought it was a person.

"We don't rent anymore so we pulled out all the shelves. I haven't seen one thing since then and I feel like it went with them. It's been a couple of years now. I don't know if it was connected to something or just the feel. Because when you go in the back room, what it feels like now, compared to back in the day of renting, it's a totally different energy. It's just not the same. It feels like that electricity is gone. It's like the magic is gone."

Below the apartment, one of the first-floor tenants of the Bledsoe Building is the West Village Market. One day, Jamie and Tonya saw something inside the market that was completely unexpected.

"There's two huge windows to West Village Market facing Haywood Road," Jamie explained. "At that time, those windows didn't have curtains and weren't all painted up. They barely had anything in there because it's just a little market joint. They had low shelves at that time and it was way more open and spacious. We were walking past the second window and Tonya looked in. I see her body language. She stiffens up. I thought she had seen herself and I started to say, 'You don't look that bad' as a joke."

"This is the weirdest thing I have ever seen," Tonya admitted. "I saw somebody inside the market. I was like, 'Wow, they're really tall,' because I was seeing them above the aisle. I saw really long black hair, a very long, extended nose, and these really long hands. I didn't see the rest of its body. It was almost like it was floating above the aisle. I didn't see a lower body, just that it was kind of smoky behind it. I felt like it was almost elemental. It didn't feel bad. I've just never seen anything like that looked like that. I was like, 'Okay, this isn't right.' Then, it looked like it started shaking. It was like it was sniffing air in and then the hands started to rattle with those really long fingers. It scared me so bad I started running."

Jamie explained, "The door that you go in to get to our apartment above the store is right there, between those glass windows. So, you have to go towards what she saw to get into our door. Tonya makes this noise and runs to the door and grabs it. At that time, I look in and I see this thing. I don't know how to describe it. There was this giant head-looking thing floating over all these tendrils coming out. It looked like a stereotypical witch's face with a big, pointy nose. It had these tentacles that looked like wood but they were flailing, moving around and touching everything, like the tops of the shelves. It looked like they were searching the area instead of just flapping or waving. I don't know if it was searching for something or wondering where it was or just checking its environment. That's the feel I got. It was really, really weird. I could see where the eyes were, I could see the nose and a mouth area, and those tendrils. I felt like it had been looking at me and it was looking away just as I looked up. I only saw it for a second, literally just long enough to know that I *did* see it. It scared me so bad. I did a double take and stepped back but it was gone. I didn't see it in there anymore but it scared the shit out of me. Then, I think, 'Something's behind me!' But it would have been out on the street. I turn around and there's nothing there.

"The door hadn't even closed yet behind Tonya. She was getting up the stairs and I went running after her. Tonya and I, we trained martial arts for years and years. My dad was a Golden Gloves boxer. He taught me how to fight when I was a kid, so I've never been worried about people. People don't scare me, even though they're the worst thing you can run into, bar none. Tonya is not a scaredy cat either. So, to see her scared and run away from something really scared the shit out of me.

"I get upstairs and she's like, 'Did you...?' and I was like, 'Shut up, shut up, shut up, shut up, shut up, shut up, shut up! Do not describe it to me! Do not say a word. Draw what you saw! Draw what you saw!' We drew the pictures and we drew almost identically the same thing! I've never seen anything like that. And not even just the way it looked, but I could *feel* it when I saw it. It felt earthy, spirit-y. Like an elemental? It didn't feel like a human. I would have never been like, 'Oh, that dude over there' or 'That lady.' It wasn't like that. I don't know how to describe it, but it was really terrifying. Even though it wasn't acting intimidating, it scared the hell out of me. Just the looks of it. It was like nothing I've ever even thought about seeing before.

"I still can't believe I saw that thing. That messed me up because that thing is positioned downstairs right under our apartment. After a while, it was so scary it was funny. I'm telling Tonya the things that I'm afraid of. I was like, 'What if it comes up here? Like you're gonna open the door it's going to be in the hallway? Oh, man, what if it comes up and gets you in the shower? You better watch out!' I'm making a joke out of it and it made me feel better but it's scaring her because it's terrifying. Tonya's like, 'Shut up!' I couldn't stop laughing. But the whole time I'm thinking, 'Oh, my God, I hope that doesn't happen!'

"It's weird because I worked near there and I go to the market all the time. I think about that thing in the market every time I go in there and I go in there sometimes twice a day. I'm always like, 'Oh, that thing was floating here.' I asked them one time if they had ever heard anything there. They said sometimes stuff gets knocked off the shelves. But I'm not going to be like, 'Oh, I saw this giant freaking thing in here!' No need to panic them. If they're not seeing anything, then it's okay."

"That's the strangest thing I've ever seen!" Tonya said. "I don't even know what that is. I don't even know what's going on. It was a lot to comprehend. I've told some people that work at the market a little bit about this. They said they do feel like there's something here."

One spirit that Tonya and Jamie encountered was much beloved by the couple.

"I do feel like we have animal spirits around," Tonya began. "On Haywood, there's the radio station 103.3. We lived underneath there for a little while."

"That's 'The Swamp'," said Jamie. "That place was horrendous. We had a bunch of mice when we moved in, and then rats moved in and ate them. And then possums moved in and ate them. Every time it rained, it would flood and form a giant puddle in the middle of the living room. It had mud and mold shooting out of the corners, up from the floor. We had to take the bed out of the bedroom because it was falling through the floor. That place was terrifying.

"The people upstairs, I swear to God, at one point they hired a centaur and Frankenstein to work up there. Unbelievable stomping and noise. I swear all they did was move furniture for four hours a day.

"The way we were living was really bad. But we couldn't move, couldn't do anything about this place. I was losing my mind. We were both really horribly depressed. But we used to see a huge dog."

"There was a spirit of a giant, white wolf," Tonya agreed. "You'd see it and you could see its face, and then it would turn around and go away, just disappear. It would just be gone!"

"It was so scary the first couple of times," Jamie admitted. "I would think there was a giant dog in the house. You would see it out of the corner of your eye and turn around to look, and there would be nothing there. But the cats would be looking. Or Tonya would be looking. This happened several times in the kitchen. Sometimes I could see its shape and shadow in the dark, like in a doorway. It would just be standing there. It was really unclear, but you could see that it was there. It was almost like TV static. Other times it would pass through the room like it was made out of smoke. It would just stop and look at me.

"I saw the dog a lot and it became a thing where it was not a surprise anymore. I was really happy to see it because I got a very distinct, friendly feel from this thing. The dog was really positive. It didn't show me anything otherwise. It made me feel very comforted. It was a trip to actually be enjoying seeing a spirit roaming around your house. I loved it and I felt like it was there because it loved us, so I talked to it. Sometimes when you talked to it, it would pop up. You'd see a little wisp of something in the room. It was amazing."

"It was really cool," Tonya told me. "It was just hanging out."

"Even the cats were okay with it, which was weird," Jamie said. "The cats would both pick their heads up and look in the same direction, like 'Did you see that?' I'm like, 'Yeah, I saw that. It was there.' But they were never afraid of it.

"When we moved, we tried our best to bring it with us. Just letting it know that we love it and we want it to be happy and be with us. I was like, 'It's okay. You can come with us. Please come with us. I don't want to leave you here in this terrible place.' I don't think that happened, unfortunately. I don't want it to be stuck there for some weird reason. Our landlord, she was horrible, so I didn't want to ask her if she knew anything about it. But I do miss that thing."

Tonya and Jamie's unusual experiences are not limited to the Asheville area. They have borne witness to the nearby phenomenon known as the Brown Mountain Lights.

"We've gone to Brown Mountain to see if we could see the lights," Tonya said. "The overlook is a little stop where trucks could pull off if they needed to. It was the best place because it was chill. We'd go up there and eat snacks, hang out. Sit on the guardrail, enjoy the sky. Sometimes we could see the lights and they were interesting to watch. They were green and they would start low on the mountain. We definitely saw them go up higher and then go up into the sky!"

"I've seen smears over the trees in a wavy pattern, almost like if you smeared light with your hands," Jamie described. "There's stuff that shoots up into the clouds that looks like fireworks."

"There were also these weird little owls that would mess with us," said Tonya.

"These hyper-aggressive birds that come out and mess with you before the sun comes up," Jamie echoed. "It's so weird. And there's the sound of chains all night moving all through the forest."

"One time, we walked out to the road where there's this guardrail," Jamie began. "All of a sudden it felt like the air got heavy. It felt like you're underwater, like it was pushing me down. I felt all this electricity and the guardrail popped, all the way down as far as we could see. You could hear the entire guardrail pop, 'GONG!!'"

"We heard this weird thumping noise like, "WHOOOOOOOOOONG!" Tonya said. "It scared us.

"It rang out and then the pressure slowly lifted off. "We were covered in static," Jamie said. "It was like the weirdest electromagnetic thing."

"I touched the guardrail and it was vibrating really hard," Tonya said. "We go running over to get into the car and wait it out a little bit longer to see if we could see some more. I don't know what that sound was. It was really loud. And I can't explain the vibration that you could feel. When we were on our way back home, when we got to Patton Avenue, my phone died and my car died all at the same time! I had just gotten the cell phone and it was fully charged and I had just got a new battery in the car. I don't know if it drained the batteries or what, because nobody really knows what's going on up there on Brown Mountain."

"If you have never gone to Brown Mountain, you need to do it," Jamie encouraged. "You want to go before the leaves come back. And go to Morganton. I've seen way more stuff on that side."

These days, ghostly activity that Jamie experiences is more subdued and his perspective on the subject is more philosophical.

"I feel like ghosts are not here to hurt you," he told me. "I've had my hair pulled. I've heard stuff talk to me. Sometimes they're not sentient enough to do anything. They're just living their un-life. I go to a lot of clubs to play music and I will see the shape of someone and turn around and they're not there. I'm not really afraid of them. It makes me feel bad for them. Are they trying to make contact? Or are they just lonely? Or they could be terrified, absolutely scared, if they don't know why they're there. Or maybe it's somebody I know that came to see me and say, 'Hello.' Not having any real connection with them upsets me.

"I've always felt like I was 'open to things', so maybe that's why things happen. Humans need the capability to say, 'Maybe I don't understand what's going on,' that relinquishes your control on the reality of things that you know for a fact, or you *think* you know for a fact. It's like nobody's willing to let go of the reins and say, 'Well, shit's happening here and maybe I don't know why, but it is actually happening,' instead of just pretending it's not happening. I'm more than willing to do that but a lot of people won't. They won't open their minds to stuff that they don't understand, because that means, 'Maybe I don't understand other things, too.' But don't ignore that something's happening. Or tell people *they're* crazy because *you* don't understand it. You don't know shit and everything could change overnight. Everything. Also, it's not an insult to have a mental issue. You know what the real problem is? Being an asshole."

Tonya believes that, even though she may be naturally inclined to experience the supernatural more often than the average person, the energy of Asheville itself is contributing to strange events that occur.

"My house is pretty quiet now. It's cool," she told me. "But I do feel like Asheville has a bunch of energy. It's not all bad. There's a lot of good energy. Something pretty strong, something special. And I do think it draws people to Asheville. But it might attract things or keep things. Stuff's not leaving. It's sticking around."

I spoke with Elle who previously lived in West Asheville and has had unusual experiences all her life.

"I am originally from Australia," Elle told me. "But I've been all over the place. I've lived all across the east coast of Australia, so Melbourne, Sydney, Brisbane. I'm a practicing occultist and I have been since my late childhood. I have had numerous encounters with spirits and entities and earth entities. At night, I would be visited by these two very tall, slender beings who would stand over my crib and stroke my head.

"When I was very young, my parents bought a property out in the country where it's very hilly, much like Appalachia. The mountainous regions are definitely my favorite. It was all dirt roads. While they started building a house, we stayed at a Bed and Breakfast close by that was an early 1800s farmstead house. The owners would rent out the entire thing so there wasn't meant to be anyone else in the house. The owners would be there, too, sometimes, during the day. But there wasn't someone's old mum also living in a back room.

"There was a room which looked like the lace section of the Joann store had thrown up in there. All the lace in the world. It was all florals and lace trimmings. A very pretty room, ultra feminine. Your grandmother would have a blast being in this room. It was gorgeous and didn't feel threatening whatsoever. There were other kids there and we were daring each other to go in that room because there was a scary lady. I remember toddling into this room and there's this beautiful window and light streaming in. I would see there's a woman sitting in the corner who isn't quite there. I can't see her face. I would shriek and run back out. It was a game. We would all do it. All the other kids could see her, too, right up to the oldest.

"My great-grandfather died. I would sometimes stay in the room that was his when visiting my great-grandmother and my grandmother. I would often hear a ragged breathing very close to my bed. At first it freaked me out, until I got the very distinct sense that it was my Dada. And then I wasn't afraid anymore."

After moving into their new home, Elle continued to experience the strange activity.

"I walked over a ridge one day," she began. "I knew the other side to be a drop off onto my neighbor's driveway. But instead of the drop off, it was a gully with a stream and fairies. I stood there in shock staring for a little while at this glittering, beautiful paradise. That was a pretty cool thing. I ran to go get my mom but by the time I got back, it had gone back to being the driveway. The scene that I saw was impossible for the area that I lived in. Even though I lived in a very green, lush area, it was high summer and high summer in Australia is a dead, dry, hot, constant fire risk. There is no green whatsoever. It couldn't have been some*where* else. It had to have been a glimpse into some*thing* else."

Elle's early experiences shaped who she was and how she interacted with everyone around her.

"I was definitely the weird kid," Elle admitted. "The other weird kids considered me to be too weird! But none of this has ever been particularly shocking to me. Those things that were happening to me as a child just seemed very normal.

"I developed clairsentient abilities as a kid, but lost them as I grew up. I think I got jaded. My abilities came back after I had a near-death experience during childbirth. I also have synesthesia. That means that my receptors are crossed. I can taste music. Sometimes I'll see emotion, that kind of thing."

Eventually, Elle made her way to the United States. She did not leave her penchant for unusual experiences behind.

"I've been in the U.S. for almost ten years," she told me. "I started off in the north but the only thing creepy that happened there was a bad marriage. I was in Wilmington, North Carolina, before this and I've been in Asheville for four years.

"My current husband was with me in Wilmington. We were just dating at the time. He doesn't often see things, but he's certainly very open. We were driving up the road one night and it was raining. As the headlights turned a corner, I can see a man's legs in white pants walking right in front of us. My husband just kept going. I started backing up in the seat and I shrieked thinking, 'Oh my gosh! He can't see them! We're about to hit someone!' We went *through* the legs. Nothing hit! Had it actually been a person, there is absolutely no way that we wouldn't have heard something. There would have been an almighty bang. It would have been terrible accident. But they just weren't there anymore.

"About year or two later, I was driving up the road and there was two cars in front of me. I caught sight of a man. He was in the middle of the road, but going left to right. He was a black man in a full white outfit, like white linen. He looked solid. A full-bodied apparition! Had he been a real person, he would have been hit. There was nowhere for him to go other than directly across the road. There's no trees that could have obscured him, absolutely nothing. Traffic was moving. He walked directly over the road, through traffic. None of the other cars reacted. No one else saw him. A car went through him and he disappeared. He didn't get into a car, anything like that. He was just gone.

"I sat there and it slowly came to me, 'That was a ghost! And it was the same ghost!' It's not just once. It's the second time this has happened. This was the same place, just going from the other direction. Now, the right-hand side of the road is the cemetery of the Zion Church. It's almost like this ghost is getting up every morning and he's going for his walk and then he goes back home the same way. I thought, 'That's really cool!'"

That was not the last time Elle had a run-in with phantom legs.

"The first experience I had in Asheville was hilarious," she began. "I was driving on Riverview Drive at Beverly Road in the late afternoon. It was slightly foggy but not foggy enough that it would obscure any actual things. Riverview Drive is built along a steep facing hill which goes down into Carrier Park and then along the train lines. It's not bush, there are a few houses there, but there's not much on the other side. You get bears and deer and all sorts of things. As I was approaching, I saw what appeared to be long dog legs crossing the road. It was coyote legs! A vision of *just legs* and they crossed from the right-hand side to the left. And it wasn't far away. It was close, probably 15 feet away. It could not have been real. There's absolutely no way that it would have been a real coyote. I rubbed my eyes thinking, 'Oh, I can't see the rest. Maybe I've got a floater in the way.' I watched for two or three seconds. The legs just kept going and then disappeared. It was just phenomenal! I thought that was pretty funny. I've never seen anything like that again.

"This was weird," she continued. "I was taking my son and my daughter for a walk on Riverview when my son was little. My son is very, very sensitive. And we were standing on the ridge on Riverview Drive when all of a sudden, he moves like he's been pushed. He said, 'Hey! He pushed me!' and he points to nothing. There's no one else on the road at all. I said, 'Who pushed you?' He said, 'There's a man right there and he's crying and he pushed me.' I said, 'Is he talking to you?' And he said, 'No, he's just crying.' I said, 'All right, well, we're going to leave now, so tell him to stay here and not to come near you again.'"

A moment later, her son spoke again: "He's following us. He wants to come home with *you*."

"I immediately was like, 'No, no, I'm not doing this. I don't need any random ghost babies.' I said, 'Don't look behind you. Leave him alone. Just don't look at him anymore.'

"We got home and I put up more protection around the house. You don't want attachment entities walking into your home. My son said for the next few days that he was at the door and he was still crying.

"I know there's a lot of heroin addicts and drug users that go up there. There's little camps and chairs right over the side of the drop off where they'll go and they'll take drugs. I'm wondering if someone overdosed there and woke up as a hungry ghost. It took a while, but he eventually moved off. We didn't hear or see him again, but that certainly was gross. It really felt quite grody."

A few years ago, Elle moved to West Asheville and her strange experiences continued.

"We got to West Asheville in 2018. The landlady was showing us around the place. It was not super old, not yesterday's or anything. Probably 1960s. But I immediately felt something.

"With every house I move into, I always ask the landlord, 'Has someone died here? Is it known to be haunted?' And I have to preface that with, 'I'm sorry, I'm just creepy. I like to know.' It gets a laugh. When I asked her that, she paused for a second. She's like, 'I don't think it's haunted. The tenant who lived here before you was a man, a firefighter. He died three years ago. He didn't die in the house, but he was found unresponsive in the house and then later died in hospital.' It turned out that this guy was the same age as us. So, if he was alive now, he would still be the same age. He and his girlfriend and their son had lived in the house. I didn't know at the time what had happened and I still don't fully know."

After moving in, Elle had a chat with the presence she felt there.

"I walked through the house. It was just me and I said, 'If there's anyone here, you're welcome to come and talk to me, but you're going to abide by the rules of my house.' I do this in every house I go to because there's always something. Even if it's not a ghost, there's something there. It felt like a very masculine presence. I said, 'Would you tell me your name?' I got the very strong sense of a B sound. I said, 'I can't really hear you, sir. Do you mind if I call you Brian?' It didn't feel bad so it's like, 'All right, cool. Brian it is.'

"He would just hang out. Like sometimes you'd walk into a room and you'd realize that Brian was there. But it wasn't creepy. He was very sweet with the kids. The kids would occasionally see him, but they were very small at the time. My daughter was eight months old. My son was 14 months older than her. You'd watch them track nothing across the room and then go back to playing.

"There was a couple of times where my daughter would wake up at night crying and I would go in to check on her. She's in her crib and the touch lamp is about five or six feet away on a side table. She could not get to it, but the touch lamp would be dimming and getting brighter and dimming and getting brighter on its own. I'd have to say, 'Brian, you've got to knock it off. You're waking up the baby.' And it would immediately stop. That was pretty funny.

"Sometimes he had a very creepy sense of humor. It was like he was trying to be a stereotypical ghost. The house had an attached garage with a workbench. I was down there at night doing some work at the workbench. I felt a very distinct presence which then whooshed right up behind me and whispered in my right ear very fast: 'Self-inflicted gunshot wound.' And then it felt like it was laughing.

"I'm standing there. I'm like, 'That's not funny. That's actually really creepy. If that's the case, I'm really sorry that that happened. But don't be weird, please! I know you had a child, too. I don't care if you mess with me. But don't scare us. Please, please be nice.'

Eventually, Elle serendipitously gained new information about "Brian."

"I was at a farmers market and the fire guys go through and make sure that everyone's tent weights are secure at the beginning of every market," she explained. "I introduced myself to them and I said, 'I live in a house on Riverview Drive and apparently one of your guys used to live there. He died within the last few years.' He said, 'It kind of rings a bell. Can you give me more info?' I described it. He's like, 'Oh, yeah,' and he gave me the name Bryce. He said that the guy had been a firefighter. Apparently, he was a joker, loved to joke. He left to become an Arctic fisherman had been injured on a boat in Alaska. He came back to Asheville, back to the house to be with his girlfriend and son, and then he died.

"His name did start with a 'B' and he was he was the right age. I didn't tell the fire chief my experiences. I just said that I'd heard that he'd lived there."

"At that stage, somebody decided that they were going to hex me," Elle declared. "I don't know why. It was some person who'd taken offense to something."

"How did you know about the hex?" I asked.

"Well, all hell broke loose in the house!" she said. "My husband, he's a chef. This was at Christmas time and he came home late, probably two or three in the morning. I was already asleep. He said that he sat up most of the night hearing knocking all through the house: the walls, the floors, the ceiling, the basement. Just this constant knocking. And disturbingly enough, it was in threes, which is not always a great sign. I had two friends come over who are somewhat sensitive and one of them was able to see something walking through the house towards my daughter's room. She was asleep at the time and our dog was in her room. All of a sudden, my daughter woke up screaming and the dog started barking like crazy.

"We had things flying off the walls. It was almost Hollywood style, like you'd imagine exorcist teams coming in. We had a decorative brass plate on the wall. I think it's Pakistani or Indian. I was standing in the kitchen and I was aware of a sound, but not concentrating on it. All of a sudden, the plate flew off the wall. It launched off the wall, probably four feet, onto the floor. I realized that, while I'd been standing in the kitchen concentrating on cooking, I'd been hearing the wire holding the plate to the hooks being repeatedly bent so that it could be broken. I must have been standing there for three or four minutes and it was taking its time, constantly doing this, until it flung itself off the wall.

"I was pissed. I started yelling at it. I was walking around and smudging and making my mark and saying, 'You can't do this. We don't have this here. You have to leave. And if you don't, I'm going to throw you into the void. I've done it before and I'll do it again.'

"It didn't find that terribly threatening, unfortunately. Probably a day later, I walked down our hall past a decorative Moroccan tile that was on the wall in a framed case. It launched itself off the wall just after I walked past.

"By that stage, I was like, 'Okay, fine, we're not doing this anymore.' So, we had to cleanse the house. My husband and I walked through and we did our own cleansing. That was awful, really unpleasant. And then to double down, we had to get the big guns out. A friend of mine put me in touch with a woman in South Carolina. She's a non-denominational exorcist and is profoundly psychic. Without knowing my address or having any pictures of my house, she described our house perfectly and told me that we'd been cursed and that we had a demonic presence. She talked to it and told it that it had to leave. Then, it left of its own volition, which was nice.

"So, whatever they sent, we were able to get rid of it. All was well once again. But, at that stage, Brian had disappeared. Because you never really know how things work on the other side, I was really worried about him for quite a while, thinking that perhaps he'd been made to leave. Or maybe he was being used horribly in some way. But he eventually came back just before we left in 2021. I wished him well and off we went."

"We've moved to Candler since then. This house was built in 1962. The family who used to live here, the mother had left but the son was still here. The father was a veteran but had died a few years before.

"In 2021, everybody's buying everything, right? The night before we found out that we'd been successful in buying it, I had a dream that a man was with me in the house. He was showing me around the whole house. When we got to the bottom of the basement stairs, he grabbed my forearm and he looked me dead in the eye. Usually when I dream, if there's people in my dreams, I don't really see facial features. If I do, I generally take that as being more of a real experience, not so much of an imaginary dream. I'm actually encountering a person. This man looked at me dead in the eye and he made me promise that I would always work on my relationship and never give up on my marriage. I promised him and he let go of my arm. He smiled and he said, 'Okay, you've got the house.'

"The very next morning, I woke up, turned my phone on, and my realtor had called and said, 'Yes, you were successful.' I thought that was lovely.

"There's not a lot of activity in this home. The man is not here, at least not that I know of. Apparently, he died of lung cancer. But my husband has said that he's woken up a few times hearing someone coughing or feeling someone press on the corner of the bed at his feet. So maybe he is here but he just comes around occasionally.

"Just a few weeks ago, my son woke me up to tell me that there was a lady in his closet and she was talking, but he couldn't hear her. This was the night of my grandmother's funeral. I went into his room and he pointed to the spot where she was. He said that she was still there and that she was still talking. I couldn't see anything but he perfectly described my grandmother at the very end of her life. I tried to take a picture and the face recognizer on my phone went off exactly where he was pointing, which I thought was pretty cool."

Considering all her strange experiences through her lifetime, Elle knows that science gives an incomplete picture of the universe around us.

"We've distanced ourselves, divorced of anything which isn't fully explainable by science and 100% material. That's quite a bland existence, especially for those of us who do not live in that realm. We can't be normal. The more that we go into this very strange time in history, more people are coming to the understanding that we're not just living in this material existence. It's not just what you can see and touch. I've had so many encounters now it's just part of the usual. None of this is foreign or strange to us."

Elle shared with me that she was excited to be featured in a book of ghost stories.

"I love this stuff!" she told me. "Growing up and finding the Time Life book on Ghosts or the Aliens one. I love those things. We've since collected all of them. I didn't realize then that everyone else had also loved them. I thought it was just me! Hopefully this will be one of those books that some other weird kid finds and is like, 'Oh, cool!' That's what we hope for, right? Any time you create something, you hope it goes to the right person."

On this, I agree with Elle wholeheartedly.

North side of Haywood Road – Commercial Building, Post Office, Palace Theatre, and Red Star Filling Station

Photo courtesy of the D. H. Ramsey Library, Special Collections, University of North Carolina at Asheville, E. M. Ball Photographic Collection (1918-1969.)

Workers relocating the streetcar tracks on Haywood Road in 1914

Photo courtesy of the North Carolina Collection, Pack Memorial Library, Asheville, North Carolina

West Asheville References

"Bledsoe Building." *Nc.gov*. https://files.nc.gov/ncdcr/nr/BN1415.pdf. National Register of Historic Places Registration Form. Accessed June 2, 2023.

Calder, Thomas. "Tuesday History: The sulphur springs of West Asheville." *Mountain Xpress*. https://mountainx.com/news/tuesday-history-the-sulphur-springs-of-west-asheville/. Published September 27, 2016. Web. Accessed June 9, 2023.

Cooper, Grady. "A shifting identity: West Asheville's storied past." *Mountain Xpress*.

https://mountainx.com/news/community-news/040214a-shifting-identity/. Posted April 3, 2014. Web. Accessed June 1, 2023.

Elle. Interview with the author.

Holderfield, Culley and Lang, Phyllis. "Haywood Road: The Story of Haywood Road." *North Carolina Ancestral Trackers*. The West Asheville Story. A Publication of the West Asheville History Project. Volume 1, Issue 1, Winter 2001. https://www.ancestraltrackers.net/nc/haywood/story-haywood-road.pdf. Web. Accessed June 12, 2023.

Jamie. Interview with the author.

Manikowski, Amy C. "Sulphur Springs." *Asheville Historic Inns*. https://ashevillehistoricinns.wordpress.com/2013/08/27/sulphur-springs/. Published August 27, 2013. Web. Accessed June 9, 2023.

Pennell, George. "Traipsin' in Historic West Asheville." *Asheville Citizen-Times*. (October 20, 1960). Sulphur Springs/Robert Henry. Newspapers.com. Retrieved June 2, 2023, from https://citizen-times.newspapers.com/article/asheville-citizen-times-sulphur-springs/23915359/.

Sanford, Jason. "For sale: Part of the Bledsoe Building on Haywood Road in West Asheville, a red-hot real estate zone." *Ashvegas*. https://ashvegas.com/for-sale-part-of-he-bledsoe-building-on-haywood-road-in-west-evillred-hot-real-estate-zone/. Posted June 13, 2014. Web. Accessed June 2, 2023.

Tonya. Interview with the author.

"West Asheville – Aycock School Historic District." *Nc.gov*. https://files.nc.gov/ncdcr/nr/BN1839.pdf. National Register of Historic Places Registration Form. Web. Accessed June 9, 2023.

"795 Haywood Road." *Buncombe County Assessment Property Record Search*. https://prc-buncombe.spatialest.com/#/property/963815208200000. Web. Accessed June 9, 2023.

Wikipedia contributors. (2022, August 17). West Asheville End of Car Line Historic District. In Wikipedia, The Free Encyclopedia. Retrieved June 2, 2023, from https://en.wikipedia.org/w/index.php?title=West_Asheville_End_of_Car_Line_Historic_District&oldid=1104988016.

THE SMITH-MCDOWELL HOUSE

The four-story Smith-McDowell House was built during the 1840s, long before the Civil War, and is the oldest standing home in Buncombe County. The house, first known as the Buck House, was built by James McConnell Smith, one of the wealthiest landowners and businessmen in Asheville. The home was situated on a plantation south of Asheville on land that James inherited from his father, Daniel, who received a land grant after the Revolutionary War. Smith eventually owned more than 30,000 acres across Buncombe County.

James Smith grew his wealth by operating a tannery, a tavern, a mercantile shop, a gold mine, and the Buck Hotel in downtown Asheville. Smith also ran a toll bridge over the French Broad River. What started out as a simple ferry later became known as "Smith's Bridge."

Travelers on the Buncombe Turnpike paid Smith a fee each time they crossed the river. Farmers bringing hogs and turkeys to market in South Carolina and Georgia had to pay for the animals' crossing as well. The bridge became very lucrative for Smith, especially since it ushered the travelers into downtown Asheville where he welcomed them to his Buck Hotel to lodge for a fee.

I had the pleasure of meeting with Lisa, a volunteer at the Smith-McDowell House who is very familiar with the building and its history. Lisa described Smith's moneymaking operation this way:

"Smith's hotel catered to such travelers with pens out back for the animals and feed corn for sale that was grown on Smith farmland. Before leaving the next morning, Smith sold them any supplies they needed. When they're off down the road to go to the next place, here comes a whole bunch more. The newspaper at the time called hog season in Asheville, 'A sea of hogs.' They are coming in and they're going out."

The Buck Hotel was located about where the A.C. Hotel is currently. Smith's Bridge was located south of the where the current Highway 240 bridge crosses the river and stood there until it washed out in the flood of 1912.

In the 1840s when James Smith began construction on his house, most buildings in Asheville were made of logs or clapboard, including his Buck Hotel. The Smith-McDowell house was the first house in Asheville built using brick and likely used enslaved laborers.

"We don't know why James Smith built the house way out here," Lisa said, "Because if you think about the 1840s, this was a far piece from town." The property originally also contained the Smith family cemetery.

James Smith and his wife Mary "Polly" Patton Smith raised their children in the home. An interesting familial side-note is that Polly's sister, Elizabeth Patton, was married to Davy Crockett. In 1849, James Smith became the second mayor of the City of Asheville. Four short years later, Polly passed away.

In 1855, James Smith passed away and bequeathed his land to his brother, John, intending for John to farm the extensive lands. John moved into the house, but died only one year later, in 1856. Because John died without a will, there was no one designated to inherited the home and land, and the entirety had to be sold at auction.

The house was sold to William Wallace McDowell who was a banker. The good news was that William McDowell was not only a previous business associate of James Smith's, but also, he was married to Sarah Lucinda Smith McDowell, who was James Smith's daughter. Thus, the home was ultimately kept in the family, after all. William purchased the house and 350 acres for $10,000.

William and Sarah lived in the house until 1880, raising nine children there. According to Lisa, they lived there through the Civil War period. McDowell organized the first group of Confederate volunteers from Western North Carolina, known as the Buncombe Riflemen. McDowell eventually achieved the rank of Major and he did survive the war.

"The reconstruction period was a little easier on a family like the McDowells," Lisa said, "because they had land available to sell to make ends meet. That's when they sold what used to be the cemetery." The occupants of the cemetery graves were relocated to another location. Allegedly.

In 1881, the house and 15 acres was sold to Alexander Garrett, an immigrant from Ireland who came to Asheville from St. Louis, Missouri.

Lisa told me, "Alexander came with his son, Robert, and Robert's wife, Mary Frances, and their young daughter, Alexandra, named for her grandfather. They came because Mary Frances had tuberculosis. This was the part of Asheville's history as a mecca for tuberculosis patients to come to Asheville. At this time, they added on a back section and attached the summer kitchen to the main house. And, they added the beautiful solarium on the back. That's where Mary Frances would go to 'take the air.' They extended the main staircase to make it more grand and elegant. Architecture wise, it's a Federalist home. But, the interior, we see it as Victorian."

Garrett also founded Victoria, a community nearby to the house that catered to the wealthy. Garrett was the Mayor of Victoria and constructed the Victoria Inn. Later, Garrett sold the home to his son, Robert, for $1.00.

In 1898, the Smith-McDowell House was sold to Dr. Charles Van Bergen and his wife, Amelia Stevenson Van Bergen, who were good friends of the Vanderbilts. In 1900, the landscaping at the home was revised based on a plan developed by famed landscape architect, Frederick Law Olmsted, Jr. Olmsted's plan included adding a carriage house and reflecting pool, in addition to beautiful gardens.

In 1908, the house was purchased by General Alfred Bates and Caroline McCorkle Bates, who used it as a summer home. They sold the property to their daughter, Henrietta Bates McKee, who was a friend of the Vanderbilts and President Roosevelt.

In 1913, the home was sold again, this time to C. Brewster Chapman. During his ownership, Chapman completed extensive renovations to the home with the help of a noted Mason, Richard Sharp Smith, who also oversaw construction at the Biltmore Estate.

Upon his death in 1920, Chapman willed the home to his friend Hermann Gudger, the Vice-President of the Goldwyn film corporation. But, Gudger never lived in the home. He only used it as a rental. After Gudger passed, the home was sold in 1951 to the Catholic diocese who used it as a school and dormitory.

Lisa explained, "When the diocese owned the home, it was used as a dormitory for up to 20 Catholic high school boys. In those four bedrooms upstairs! We've heard crazy stories about those boys. They were just here to get in as much trouble as they could and still pass."

Lisa indicated that after the school boys departed, the building was abandoned for twenty years. "From about '63 to '81, this place sat empty. I've heard stories from former Asheville Catholic High School students that remember when this was empty. They said that every now and then they'd find a window or a door open and people had gotten in. I'm surprised they had any windows left by the time that was over."

When Lisa told me that the most recent previous occupants were high school boys, I marveled that the building was still standing, let alone in the beautiful condition in which it now appears.

"I think part of its staying power is that it's made of brick," Lisa suggested. "And, it is not only exterior brick work. All the interior walls are solid brick. See the thick doorways? That's because those walls are brick. In fact, the last personal owner of the house, C. Brewster Chapman, he put a red Vermont slate roof on this house in about 1913. Although that's a very, very heavy kind of roof, this house can support it."

By 1974, the church was looking to sell the Smith-McDowell House. It was purchased by neighboring Asheville Buncombe Technical Community College.

Lisa related to me that it was the great-granddaughter of William Wallace McDowell who helped to save the house. "She was an older lady and taking Continuing Ed classes on campus," she said. "When she had to write a research paper, she wrote it about this house! She found the whole lineage of who lived here and when. Between the great-granddaughter and the Western North Carolina Historical Association, they got the house listed on the National Register of Historic Places and were able to start fundraising for restorations. You can't just allow the campus, who owned it at that time, to turn it into a parking lot!"

Also, in 1974, the Western North Carolina Historical Association saved the dilapidated home from the wrecking ball by negotiating a lease and it was restored over a six-year period.

"The historical association was working really hard to restore this place," Lisa told me. "They were bringing in plasterers and repairing things. The restoration work also included projects completed by students at Asheville Buncombe Tech. They hung wallpaper and learned faux treatments, things like that." She gestured to the lovely stamp and stencil work on the walls and ceilings of the room we were in.

"There's an active preservation society that have a say in restoration plans. And, the state has a say in it," Lisa assured me. "Whenever you do something major, it's gotta be done right. We planned colors and wallpapers aiming to reflect the period of the 1840s to 1890s, covering the era of the first three families that lived in the house. The teacher they hired through the A-B Tech program, he was an expert in all that."

The Smith-McDowell House reopened to the public as a non-profit house museum in 1981. Today, the restored Smith-McDowell House is the finest surviving example of brick antebellum architecture in Western North Carolina.

Lisa took me on a guided tour of the Smith-McDowell House and pointed out highlights of the treasures within. For example, the dining room displays a sideboard that was a wedding gift from Polly's father. In the basement, Lisa showed me a low chair that was made by one of the McDowells.

I mentioned that I was impressed with all the historic items displayed in the basement. "These are all Western North Carolina artifacts," she told me. "We think this was the 1840s winter kitchen," she continued. "We really don't know for sure, but it makes sense in a house that does have a basement. That was a typical thing to do. Take all of your summer kitchen stuff and bring it down here and utilize the extra heat that you're creating."

A musket displayed upstairs belonged to James' father. "That was used in the Revolutionary War," Lisa told me. "He did fight in the Battle of Kings Mountain. The reason it's so long is because this is a musket, not a rifle. When the bullet goes down the long tube, it bounces as it goes down. As it travels, it gets more stability. By the time it leaves the weapon, you're likely to hit whatever you've aimed at. Later, they discovered rifling, where they score a spiral down the tube. In a shorter amount of space, the bullet can spin instead of bouncing around. Then, you've got more accuracy in a shorter amount of space."

I asked Lisa how did it come to pass that the gun got saved to be displayed. She credited the southern tradition of passing down firearms through the family. "It eventually became James's property," she said.

"Then, I think his brother Jesse got it. When the family decided to quit passing it down, they took it to the library. The library had it for a long time and later transferred it over to us. These families were real good about passing stuff down. There's even James Smith's first dollar displayed here. As it got passed down, they even marked down who got it. The lady who was the last one to receive it was the great-granddaughter that helped save the house. Now, we have it."

Also on display is the Navy Colt pistol that James Smith carried with him during the Civil War. Up more stairs, the 1850s bedroom contains additional McDowell chairs and fireplace andirons. A red rocking chair from the Smith family sits next to a wooden cradle made by James Smith.

When the conversation turned to the subject of ghosts at the Smith-McDowell House, Lisa indicated that guests do have questions.

"People ask me who died here," Lisa said. "I was told that one of Mr. McDowell's brothers was recuperating from an illness and died while he was here. We know that Mary Frances died, probably here in the house. Chapman did not die here. We wish Chapman had died in this house! I hate to glorify someone's death, but it was a mysterious death. He was in a hotel in Canada. One of the maids found him in a tub of running hot water and he was in his underwear. I always thought she found him dead, but I was reading later that he died after they got him to the hospital. The Canadian Mounties still consider it an open case."

Regardless of evidence about persons dying on the property, it seems that people who spend time there do have experiences they cannot explain, including Lisa herself.

"My first experience here was very soon after I started working here, in 2006. Maybe in the first four months or so." she related. "I was upstairs at my desk. The manager was across the room and a male volunteer was down here. I was just sitting there doing my work and I hear what sounds like the voice of someone who might be standing on the staircase leading up to the office. It was a female voice. It just said, 'Lisa', nothing else.

"I thought, 'Did I hear that? Or, did I not? If it's anybody, they'll come on up around the corner.' Well, nobody ever came around the corner. I didn't hear any footsteps at all. So, I asked the manager, 'Did you call me?' She said 'No.' Anyway, she was over there and the voice came from the complete other side of me.

"The volunteer could not have sounded like that. I know him and he would not have done that. Plus, I would have heard his footsteps. I thought, 'I think I'm supposed to be creeped out, but, I'm not.' I was kind of surprised at myself that I wasn't afraid of opening the next day. I was the first person to come in and unlock the next morning. Didn't bother me in the least. This house has never bothered me. That's why I say that, apparently, this place has good vibes. I wasn't scared at all. I was intrigued. I wanted to know where it came from. That was my first paranormal experience ever."

Lisa continued, "The next experience I had was around January or February of 2007. It was during a paranormal group investigation. In my early years here, they allowed public investigations. We had 50 people coming into this house paying something like 50 bucks apiece to come in late at night and investigate. A local paranormal investigation club in town led it. It was so much fun! This event was the first time they sold tickets for the public to come in and investigate the house. It was my first foray into investigations. I wasn't even watching *Ghost Hunters* at the time! My sister was a big fan and she came up for the investigation. I learned a lot from her and I learned a lot from the investigation group about how you're supposed to act and what you're supposed to do during an investigation. It was cold, so we had to remember that if we heard a few bumps and clanks, it could be the boiler heater.

"My sister brought her equipment, camera, and tape recorder. She and I were sitting on the couch in the parlor with three recorders. It was really late and very, very quiet. You couldn't hear any of the other people in the house. Some people might have already left. My sister asked me who we usually associate with this particular room. As I am wont to do, I started my answer with, 'Um...'. And, on the recording in that space between 'Um...' and answering her with the name 'Garret', there is a whisper on that recording. The whisper says, 'Garrett.' We didn't find it till we came home. I couldn't believe we actually captured something and I could hear it! I could understand it!"

I remarked that the voice also verified that their association of that room with the Garrett family was correct.

Another investigation group had cameras rolling in the house overnight. They got footage of a ball that was a trigger-object that moved from where it was originally placed. "But I like to debunk," Lisa clarified.

"And, these are very uneven floors. Did the heat come on, create a little bit of air, and move that? I'm always questioning."

Lisa related an ominous story about another early investigation conducted in the house.

"There was a young girl on one of those investigations around 2007," she said. "She was a teenager in high school. She had an experience down in the basement that was so powerful, she passed out. They had to tote her out of here! To this day, she will not go downstairs. I can't send her down there to get a chair. I can't send her down there to turn the light off. She ain't going down there anymore."

Lisa recalled seeing something strange during one investigation. "I watched one person put their hand near a cradle we have that was made by James Smith. She felt a pull. And I watched her move a little bit with that pull."

A woman and her grandson visited the Smith-McDowell house on several occasions in 2009 to conduct their own paranormal investigations. They used dowsing rods, pendulums, voice recorders, electromagnetic field (EMF) detectors, trigger objects, and more. Over time, they did get results on the dowsing rods in several locations through the house, including the basement. The EMF detector responded near Mr. McDowell's desk. When using a rubber ball as a trigger object, the ball first rolled a great distance, stopped, and then started back up again on its own. Later, the ball rolled over the stair landing.

"It rolls off and bounces down the stairs," Lisa said. "And this is a 'super ball'. You know how they gather inertia every time they hit? It's bouncing down the stairs and I'm thinking, 'Oh, gosh, we're to find that down on the first floor.'"

Lisa later checked the recording to count: the ball bounced 9 times. "It was good to be able to go back to the recording to count: One, two, three, four.... You could hear it, Dum Dum Dum Dum.... When they went downstairs, they expected to find the ball in a far-flung spot on the floor below. To their surprise, the ball had come to a dead stop in a corner on the top of the last step. It had never even reached the floor.

"I thought that was really, really weird," Lisa concluded.

Several Electronic Voice Phenomena (EVPs) were detected. The woman asked if a little boy spirit was tired of playing alone, and an EVP response said, "By myself." Another time, an EVP seemed to say,

"McDowell." The strangest EVP was one that was not even heard when the recording was first listened to. But, when played again later, a loud voice was heard mumbling and saying the word, "cranky."

Lisa told me that the Smith-McDowell House no longer allows people to conduct paranormal investigations at the house. "We had some interesting times," Lisa said somewhat wistfully. "But the board didn't want to be known as the 'Ghost House,' so we got out of doing that."

According to Lisa, members of Campus Security have confided in her about spooky experiences at the house and in the area. "They say they see a little ghost girl playing around the front yard over at Fernihurst. They also say that they can sit down here at night and watch our lights turn on and off. I like to debunk, so I'm still trying to figure how that happens.

"We have automatic lights. I asked them, 'Is it usually on the second floor?' 'Yeah.' Well, we have automatic lights up there. They're triggered by movement. But, you know, it could be a stink bug. It could be anything crawling across the sensor. It's just every now and then, they'll see one come on. Or, they'll drive up and it's on and they'll see it go off."

Some employees express confusion when lights that they swear were turned off are found turned back on again. Lisa has experienced this phenomenon herself.

"Every time I turn off the lights in the basement, I always speak: 'Hey. How are you doing? We had a busy day; we had a slow day.' And, I turn off the light. I'm positive I did that. I'm told that's the reason nothing manifests itself to me down there, because I've acknowledged it.

"One night, I swear I turned off the basement light. And, it's not on a motion detector. My husband met me here at the house before we went to an event in Asheville. Afterwards, we came back here to pick up the second car. The light was on. My husband said, 'What are you going to do?' I said, 'I'm gonna go down there and turn the light off!' 'Really?' 'Yes!'

"We came in and he waited in the back. I got a few lights turned on so I can see what I'm doing. I go down to the basement and the light switch is flipped up. I turned the light off and we left."

Lisa is not the only one associated with the house to have a strange experience. "The spouse of one of our directors was a sensitive," Lisa confided. "Nearly every time they came here, they saw a dark shadow down the basement stairs."

Strange things happen at the Smith-McDowell house at times other than during paranormal investigations. Sometimes, events cannot be explained that happen during normal museum routines.

"We used to do a mourning exhibit," Lisa explained. "We did it during the fall for three or four years. We tied black ribbons to all the light fixtures. We covered all the mirrors."

Lisa said that the mourning exhibit was meant to show visitors the way people would have handled bodies after someone's passing during that time period.

"You're not calling the funeral director," she stated, "Things would have been done within the house. You clean the body; you get it ready. That first year, we had a 'body' upstairs. Another year, we put the 'body' down in the basement to talk about how you would have taken a body down there to clean it.

"In the parlor, we had a real wicker casket and lots of silk flower arrangements that Michael's and A.C. Moore had done for us. We had several people comment on how it smelled like flowers in that room.

"My husband came in. I hadn't told him about these other experiences. He said, 'It smells like a funeral parlor in here! I know those are fake flowers. How do you get it to smell like flowers?' Even after we took down the mourning exhibit, he smelled the flowers again. But I never smelled it. Never.

"During the 1860s, the McDowells did lose a child. In the other parlor, we had a child's coffin. We had flowers in there, too, but nobody ever talked about the flower smell up there like they did down here.

"We had mourning clothes displayed. There were panels of postmortem photography, like a father holding his dead child. There was one panel that was mostly parents and family and children. The creepiest one was where apparently the baby had died. They've got a dead baby propped up on this big, tall pedestal with a pillow down at the bottom of it. Big sister is kneeling on the pillow with her hands folded, and dead sibling up there."

I told Lisa that when I have previously talked to people about house museums, it seems that costumed re-enactments tend to stir up paranormal activity.

"When I came here in 2006, they were just finishing up a Save America's Treasure grant. So, there had been a lot of restoration activity going on. That work could have stirred something up. But we've not done anything like that since. Maybe that's why it was active then, but it's not so active now. I always expect every time we decorate for Christmas, that it may stir something up. But, it doesn't. Not that I've experienced. Lately, ghost-wise and experience-wise, the house has been dead, for lack of a better word," Lisa punned.

Regarding her past experiences, Lisa has no misgivings. "I have not felt anything in this house but good vibes," she said. "So, if they're here, they're good."

The Smith-McDowell House Museum is located at 283 Victoria Road in Asheville, North Carolina. At the time of publication, it was undergoing renovations with plans to re-open in fall 2023. For details, visit https://www.ashevillehistory.org/.

NOTE: The Smith-McDowell House no longer allows ghost hunting investigations. Please do not trouble them by asking them to do so. They are happy for you to visit for a regular tour, but, paranormal investigations are not currently allowed.

The earliest known image of the Smith-McDowell House (Buck House) taken in the early 1870s

Photo Courtesy of the Smith-McDowell House/WNC Historical Association

The Smith-McDowell House

The Smith-McDowell House, current day

Photo of William Wallace McDowell in his Confederate Officer's uniform

Photo courtesy of the Smith-McDowell House/WNC Historical Association

The room with the cradle made by James Smith where an investigator was pulled by something unseen

Smith-McDowell House References

"An Architectural Orientation to the Smith-McDowell House." *Wnchistory.org.* http://www.wnchistory.org/museum/architecture.htm. Web. Accessed May 3, 2020

Asheville Daily Citizen. Saturday Evening February 5, 1898. Page 6. https://newspapers.digitalnc.org/lccn/sn91068076/1898-02-05/ed-1/seq-6/. Web. Accessed May 3, 2020.

"Daniel Smith Cabin Location: Asheville, North Carolina." *Asheville and Buncombe County.* http://ashevilleandbuncombecounty.blogspot.com/2019/06/danlel-smith-cabin-location-asheville.html. Posted Saturday, June 15,2019. Web. Accessed January 10, 2020.

"If These Walls Could Talk: A History of the Smith-McDowell House." *Wnchistory.org.* http://wnchistory.org/museum/history.htm. Web. Accessed May 3, 2020

Lisa, a Smith-McDowell House volunteer. Interview with the author.

Lisa, a Smith-McDowell House volunteer. "Paranormal Experiences." A document about her experiences at the Smith-McDowell House.

Parris, Joyce Justus. *The History of Asheville-Buncombe Technical Community College, North Carolina.* Marceline (Missouri): Walsworth Publishing, 1996, pp. 7-8.

"Smith-McDowell House." *National Park Service.* https://www.nps.gov/nr/travel/asheville/smi.htm. Web. Accessed January 10, 2020.

The Miles Building

The edifice known as the Miles Building at the corner of Haywood and College streets is a central component of downtown Asheville. It was originally built by the Asheville Club, a social gathering place exclusively for the men of Asheville that was founded in 1881.

The building was designed by noted Mason and architect, Richard Sharp Smith. It was built on land owned by one of the Asheville Club's members, Tench Francis Coxe. Other notable members included Asheville luminaries such as Edwin Grove, James Eugene Rankin, and Edwin Carrier.

An article in the Oct. 23, 1901 edition of The Asheville Citizen previewed the building about to open for business. It described that the Miles building had two chimneys, an open upper porch, and wood pillars at the entry. The rear gave convenient access to the Battery Park roadway. Oak doors and wide stairways led to reading rooms, writing rooms, sitting rooms, and a billiard room with electric lights. Members could lounge in leather armchairs surrounded by paneled walls. The third floor housed six bedrooms and two bathrooms for members who needed overnight accommodations.

The first floor of the building was occupied by physicians offices, including the office of Dr. S. Westray Battle. Battle was a surgeon helping the many tuberculosis patients that flocked to the Asheville area for restorative air. He conducted surgery on patients in the same building. Battle was a real character on the Asheville scene. In his article, "The Long Goodbye," Steve Rasmussen described Battle this way:

"Wearing a cape, the courtly Dr. Battle would stroll the city's wooden sidewalks with a cane in one hand and a bouquet of flowers in the other -- one of which he would present with a bow to each lady he met, regardless of her social station. What truly won the good doctor a warm place in the town's heart, however, was the applejack he brewed up according to his personal recipe for the club's popular annual feast. He would serve it himself to each eager guest from a crystal punch bowl in the club's billiard room."

The Asheville Club occupied the building until 1915 and, after relocating several more times, the club shut down permanently in 1934.

Herbert Delahaye Miles was a vice president of the Armour meat packing company in Chicago when his wife contracted tuberculosis. On her doctor's recommendation, they moved to Asheville for her treatment. In 1919, Herbert Miles bought the downtown Asheville Club building from the estate of Tenche Coxe. Miles set about renovating the property to be used as office and retail spaces. By the late 1920s, the transformation was complete. Longtime tenants on the first floor included Fater's Cigar Store, and the Asheville Downtown Club, which was not related to the previous building tenant, the old Asheville Club.

A mustard and silver paint scheme on the building's interior dated from the 1920 remodel. It was touched up through the years by the descendants of the original painter. In the '50s, the original painter's son, Bill, refreshed the work. Bill's daughter, Billie, came to paint in the '80s and again in the early 2000s.

Herbert's son, Holbert Delahaye Miles, joined the family business in 1937 to assist with management of the Miles Building. Holbert's son, Elwood Miles, was born in 1942 and played in the office where his father and grandfather worked at a double-sided desk.

When Herbert Miles passed away in 1958, his will bequeathed the Miles Building to a family trust. In 1971, young Elwood followed with family tradition and came to work at the Miles building and overseeing the trust.

In 2005, Elwood Miles wanted to retire, but didn't want to sell the historic Miles Building to out-of-state investors who wanted to build condos. And, he didn't want the building torn down or his tenants evicted. Finding a suitable buyer turned out to be a tall order. Then, Miles received an offer from Stephen and Mary Ann West, newlyweds that lived near the Miles Building who were looking to make an investment. Though their offer was lower than others, Miles trusted their pledge to leave the building exactly as it was. He was more interested in a buyer's intention than ability to make the highest offer. On July 8, 2005, Elwood Miles accepted the West's offer of nearly two million dollars and sold the office building. This marked the first time in three generations that the Miles family did not own it.

The Asheville Mountain Xpress publication was founded in 1994 and, at its inception, set up shop in the Miles Building. Mountain Xpress Publisher Jeff Fobes now maintains an office in the Miles Building where a scene once unfolded that left a permanent mark on the location. It was not the result of an ancient argument between long-forgotten combatants. This event took place in the relatively recent early 1980s, when the offices were rented by a meat-packer's union.

Photographer Otis Ware also rented an office in the building. His was located across the hall from 212-213, a two-room suite next door to the former Miles' office. Ware worked late one evening and heard a woman screaming from the union office across the way. When he went to investigate the sound, Ware saw the woman being attacked. He rushed back to his office and pulled a revolver from his desk. When the attacker tried to escape, Ware fired the gun to keep the man pinned down. The criminal was eventually captured and Ware given a commendation from the mayor for his efforts. The police saw fit to subject Ware to some good-natured heckling for shooting up his landlord's property. A bullet from the event is now permanently lodged in the ceiling of Jeff Fobes office.

Putting his days as a gunslinger behind him, Ware became a Reverend and leader in the Black community, founding a church and assisting to open one of the first Black-operated radio stations in the country. The station was located in the Miles Building below Ware's photography studio.

You might suspect that gunfire was the strangest event to unfold in the Mountain Xpress office. But, with its history spanning more than 100 years, the Miles Building has seen countless people living their lives within its walls. It seems that some of those folks are hesitant to leave, even after their earthly departure. During the 26 years occupying the building, Xpress employees sometimes witness events that they cannot explain.

Rasmussen's article also details some of these strange events, saying they usually occur in Room 212-213, a suite of rooms now occupied by the Mountain Xpress Production Department. He writes:

> "When Technologies Manager Michael Ropicki joined Xpress in 1999, he and the production manager both had desks in the front room. 'It was right about lunchtime,' Ropicki recalls. 'One or the other of us had just bought lunch and brought it back and had laid a sandwich out on the desk. At exactly the same time, she and I both saw out of the corner of our eye a man's hand with a white-cuffed shirt sleeve reaching across the desk toward that sandwich. And we both looked back, thinking that it was [someone] playing some kind of a joke -- but there was no one there.'
> Arts & Entertainment Editor Melanie McGee, meanwhile, tells of having been in the front room at times 'when I know that there's nobody in the other one -- early in the morning or later at night. And sometimes I can hear the creak and the swivel of the chair in the back room. It's like the sound that a swivel chair makes when somebody gets up off of it. You know, like a metallic 'squeak-squonk' -- I've heard that several times,' she says.'"

Rasmussen interviewed Elwood Miles for the article and he revealed that he had never had a ghostly experience in the building. Miles told Rasmussen: "My father always said of people in the building that 'no one stays here forever.' He said, 'Some may stay six months, and others may stay 20 years, but nobody stays forever.'"

The spectral inhabitants of the office building might contradict his assertion.

THE MILES BUILDING IS LOCATED AT 2 WALL STREET IN DOWNTOWN ASHEVILLE, NORTH CAROLINA. IT IS PRIVATE PROPERTY, SO PLEASE BE RESPECTFUL OF THE PROPERTY AND CURRENT TENANTS.

Miles Building References

Calder, Thomas. "Asheville Archives: The Asheville Club moves to Haywood Street, 1901." *Mountain Xpress*. https://mountainx.com/news/tuesday-history-the-asheville-club-moves-to-haywood-street-1901/. Posted on September 19, 2017. Web. Accessed on March 9, 2020.

Rasmussen, Steve. "The Long Goodbye." https://mountainx.com/news/community-news/0810miles-php/. *Mountain Xpress*. Posted on August 10, 2005. Web. Accessed on March 9, 2020.

STONEHAVEN: THE BYNUM HOUSE

In 1618, William Hampton sailed from England to settle in Jamestown and do his part to settle the "New World." Hampton descendants settled in Virginia and Anthony Hampton was born there in 1715. The family later migrated to Surry County in North Carolina. Anthony married Elizabeth Preston in 1741 and together they raised six children in the Spartanburg district on the Tiger River in South Carolina. It was there on the family farm where a violent tragedy befell them.

As war with England became imminent, Anthony Hampton's neighbors delegated him, along with his sons, Edward and Preston, to persuade the Cherokees who inhabited the frontiers of the Carolinas to remain neutral in the colonists' conflict with the British during the coming war. Unbeknownst to the settlers, the British had already met with the Cherokees and come to an agreement of their own for a two-pronged attack in the upper part of the state. Leaving the meeting with an awareness of the Cherokees' ill intent, Edward and Preston rushed home to warn their family that the Cherokees were likely to attack. But it was too late.

In July of 1776, the Cherokees attacked the family, killing Anthony and his wife, Edward, Preston, and an infant child. Fortunately, daughter Margaret Hampton and her husband Gray Bynum were in North Carolina during the attack, but their eight-year-old son, John Bynum, was on the premises. John Bynum survived the attack but was captured and held captive for a year.

A descendant in John Bynum's family, Curtis Bynum, was born in 1882 and graduated from the University of Chicago School of Law in

1917. But before his career could take off, a doctor broke the news that he was going blind and recommended that Bynum take up farming. With a partner, he purchased the White Pine Creameries located at 252 Patton Avenue in Asheville. Bynum found success with the dairy and eventually started the Farmers Federation Collection System which was a pickup service that brought milk from small local dairies to a central processing plant.

In the 1920s, the government was looking to build a tuberculosis sanitarium and sought to locate it near a reliable source for a large supply of milk to be used in a new form of therapy. Bynum's creamery committed to the project and the Oteen Sanitarium was built just outside Asheville, later known as the Oteen Veterans Administration Hospital. The new sanitarium helped bring Asheville to the forefront as a national tuberculosis treatment center.

Curtis Bynum sought to build a home not far from his downtown dairy business for himself, wife Florence Helen Boyd Bynum, and their young daughter, Katherine. In 1920, a realtor took Curtis and three-year-old Katherine to visit a property on Macon Avenue just north of town and adjacent to the Grove Park Inn. In fact, the three-acre parcel was part of the Grove family land. When Bynum purchased the property, it was the first time any Grove land was sold outside the family.

Bynum commissioned Asheville architect Ronald Greene to design and build a French Norman style home. Greene also designed the Tudor Revival style Kenilworth Inn II and Asheville's first downtown skyscraper, the Gothic Revival style Jackson Building. The stone-clad Bynum House, also known as Stonehaven, was dedicated on July 5, 1923.

Katherine Bynum grew up at Stonehaven, attending schools locally and spending summers assisting with local Girl Scouts troops. During 1931, she was a member of the American Association of University Women (AAUW) and began a summer day camp for Girl Scouts. She married and eventually moved to Aurora, Illinois, where she was president of the AAUW. Katherine returned to Asheville in 1983.

In later years, Katherine's brother William took up residence at Stonehaven, followed by his son, William Bynum, Jr. During the time that William Junior, as he was known, lived at Stonehaven, he married a woman named Leila and adopted her daughter, Christina. I spoke with Christina Bynum Chivalier about her time spent at Stonehaven while she was growing up.

"My maiden name is Bynum," she explained. "My step dad married my mom and he adopted me when I was seven. That was his family who built the house. It was the first house built on that road. His parents lived at Stonehaven. After his dad passed away, we had to move there to take care of his mom. I loved his mom; she was my grandmother. We moved there in '91.

"I do remember getting told that when they were building the house, the raw the stone was having to come from the gorge, having to come that far. If you look at the front of the house, there's two 'X's, Roman numerals, above the door blending with the rock. That's the date, 1920. When I lived there, you couldn't see the golf course from the house. There were trees out there. There was also a pond and a bridge towards the top near where the WLOS TV station used to be, which is apartments now.

"It has a spiral, Cinderella staircase that goes to the center hallway of the house. That's where all four main bedrooms of the house were. The garage is so small that you couldn't even fit our cars today in there. You wouldn't be able to get out of the doors! When we first moved there, they were redoing the back patio and me and my brother were able to put in a time capsule. It's just sitting there! I remember exactly which stone it is, what it looks like.

"It had an elevator inside. That was fun to be able to push the buttons and not have to walk up and down the stairs. It has a secret safe behind a wall. It was cool. It was a fun place to grow up. You had people that wanted to be your friend just because of that place."

Fun features aside, Christina sometimes found the house to be an unsettling place to live.

"It was a nice house to live in, but it was creepy," she admitted. "If you picture the way it was when we first moved in, before we had done any renovations at all, it was dark red curtains, gold-ish brown walls. So, it was already spooky to any 14-year-old that was going to live there. Lights would come on or flicker, but I just chalk that up to old electricity. I know William's dad passed away there. His mom passed away there. I'm pretty sure a lot of people actually passed away within the house.

"I have read that the Pink Lady from Grove Park Inn has been seen roaming around the area. I've never seen anything like that. But you could feel the presence of things. Like in the main hallway in the upstairs, in between all the rooms. Anywhere you would go alone, there was a feeling like you shouldn't be there. Feeling people staring at you. You'd be in a rush to get out of that room. I got used to the fact that they were around. I'd think, 'Oh, whatever. I'll just walk a little bit faster through the hallway.'

"I slept with my door closed. It felt like you couldn't have them open for some reason. I can't say somebody or something was watching me because you didn't see somebody. I don't know how to explain it other than it was a weird feeling. But now I sleep with the doors open and it's fine."

I told Christina it sounded like there was activity, not just in one place, but throughout the house.

"Oh yeah," she agreed. "A lot of it was in the basement and bedroom area. That would be more spookier than anything. When I was 16, we put a pool table and jacuzzi in the basement. I'd use it when friends from high school came over. When you're down there with other people, it wasn't as scary. But by myself, don't get me wrong, it was a little bit scary."

Christina told me that her mother eventually admitted that she'd had strange experiences in the house, also.

"My mom stated to me at one point she came through the hallway upstairs where there was a bookcase, and that books came out at her. As far as I know, that only happened just the one time. I've never had that happen. But the stairs come out right where my mom said those books came at her and I slid down those stairs quite often. I fell down them half of the time.

"I was there until '98. As soon as him and my mom split up, he sold it for $1.4 million and never looked back. He said his past was his past and he wanted to live in Florida. He didn't even want me in his life. That house was his past, too, so he got rid of it as well."

William Bynum, Jr. sold to the property to Grove Park Inn in 1999. Oddly, Junior is often quoted as saying, "There were too many ghosts in the house for comfort."

"From what I hear, they bought it to make it into a Bed and Breakfast," Christina explained. "I just hate that he sold it and got rid of it," Christina said. "I wish I could take my kids to see the inside of it."

"Currently, there is no Certificate of Occupancy for the Bynum House, as it has stood empty for too many years and is now in such poor condition structurally," said Tracey Johnston-Crum, spokeswoman for the Omni Grove Park Inn. "We would very much like to restore and utilize the home to better serve our guests, but at this time it is not economically feasible to do so. We will continue to maintain the home's exterior and property to the best of our abilities, in order to preserve it for the neighborhood as long as possible."

Though its future is uncertain, Stonehaven may yet be inhabited by spirits of the past. Omni Grove Park Inn employee Klara Hines has heard rumors of strange activity that continues at the Bynum House.

"What I've been hearing from the security guards is that when they do checks, they will go and turn the lights off," Klara began. "Then, a few hours later, the light is back on. I don't know if it's an electrical issue. Though the building is not currently used by the inn, it does have electricity. Apparently, as evidenced by the frequency of the lights that go off and on, the ghosts are the only ones running up the power bill."

STONEHAVEN IS PRIVATE PROPERTY OWNED BY THE OMNI GROVE PARK INN AND TRESPASSING IS NOT ALLOWED.

Stonehaven: The Curtis Bynum House

A still from "Curtis Bynum House - Stonehaven, Asheville, North Carolina" by Craig Cline
https://www.youtube.com/watch?v=loxKz9wb2p4&t=2s

Stonehaven: The Bynum House

Stonehaven: The Curtis Bynum House (rear façade)

The Grove Park Inn on the left and Stonehaven (Bynum House) on the right (1924)

A still from "Curtis Bynum House - Stonehaven, Asheville, North Carolina" by Craig Cline
https://www.youtube.com/watch?v=loxKz9wb2p4&t=2s

Stonehaven: The Bynum House

Curtis Bynum

Sumner, William Hoke, Jr., 1912-1993. "Curtis Bynum at Office Desk." Negatives, J. Murrey Atkins Library Special Collections and University Archives, University of North Carolina at Charlotte, 1946-01. JSTOR, https://jstor.org/stable/community.33080774. Accessed 10 May 2023.

Stonehaven: The Bynum House References

Boyle, John. "Answer Man: No plans for historic Bynum house? New Verizon?" *Citizen Times*. https://www.citizen-times.com/story/news/local/2016/04/25/answer-man-no-plans-historic-bynum-house-new-verizon/83491268/. Published April 25, 2016. Web. Accessed May 8, 2023.

Chivalier, Christina Bynum. Interview with the author.

Dixon, Susan. "The Hampton Massacre: July, 1776." *Ychistory.org*. S.C. Biography Hampton Family. 06-30-1940. https://dspace.ychistory.org/bitstream/handle/11030/69958/00000601.pdf?sequence=1. Web. Accessed May 9, 2023.

Hines, Klara. Interview with the author.

"Sunset Terrace Historic District." *Living Places*. https://www.livingplaces.com/NC/Buncombe_County/Asheville_City/Sunset_Terrace_Historic_District.html. Web. Accessed 08 May 2023.

HELEN'S BRIDGE AND ZEALANDIA

If you mention the phrase "Zealandia Bridge" to Asheville locals, a few might have heard the name and fewer still could actually place it. But, when you say the name "Helen's Bridge," most locals can quote the rumors chapter and verse and then give you directions to get there. Helen's Bridge crosses College Street near downtown Asheville. It was originally known as Zealandia Bridge because it provided carriages access to the structure known as "Zealandia Castle" on Beaucatcher mountain.

John Evans Brown was not born in Asheville, but he lived there as his father amassed a great deal of land and built wealth by mining mica. In 1849, Brown left Asheville to join the Gold Rush out west. When that adventure was not successful, he traveled to New Zealand where he raised sheep and became a politician. Brown returned to Asheville in 1888 to settle for good and began construction on Zealandia Castle. While Vanderbilt began construction on the Biltmore Estate across town, Brown was building his mansion on 13 acres closer to downtown Asheville. Brown named his castle "Zealandia" in honor of the country that was his home for 30 years. It was a pebbledash-on-brick style structure that was supposedly based on Haddon Hall in England. In 1895, not long after construction was complete, Brown died at age 68 and was buried in Asheville's Riverside Cemetery.

Zealandia was purchased in 1903 by Australian diplomat Sir Philip S. Henry. Henry's wife, Violet, had recently been killed in the tragic Windsor Hotel fire in New York City. Warned about the fire by hotel staff, Violet rushed outside, but upon remembering some valuable jewelry she'd left behind, she returned inside. The fire had already weakened the structure and ceiling collapsed, killing her. Philip Henry then made the journey to Asheville alone.

Henry hired Biltmore field architect Richard Sharp Smith to expand the structure. Smith, who also designed All Souls Cathedral in Biltmore Village, designed the quarried stonework bridge that Henry added to the carriageway in 1909. After Henry's expansion, the home became a 62-room, three-story Tudor Revival, including wrought-iron entrance gates, a three-story porte cochere, and massive chimneys.

Henry died in 1933 and the property was inherited by his daughters, Violet and Lenore. The girls used Zealandia to host members of the Air Force as an Officer's Club during World War II. Lenore's husband was killed in the war and she sold her part of Zealandia to Violet.

In the 1950s, Violet was not keen on the older portions of the castle that had been built by Brown, and some of it was in bad disrepair. After they removed these sections, as well as to some of the 1908 addition, only 28 rooms remained.

Violet sold the property out of the family for the first time to a couple named Dixon. The Dixons' primary residence was in Miami, but they visited Asheville during the year. They had an art collection that included Marie Antoinette's bed and a throne that belonged to the emperor Maximilian.

On March 14, 1977, the structure remaining of Zealandia Castle was added to the National Register of Historic Places. In 2004, the property was purchased by Zealandia Holding Company, a vacation resort business that is restoring and preserving the historic property.

Zealandia Bridge required additional support to protect it from destruction when the Department of Transportation was blasting nearby to create the Tunnel Road tunnel. The supports did their job, but time took its toll. In 1998, the city considered demolishing the crumbling structure. Preservationists persevered, and the bridge remained. Now, it is structurally sound and being considered to be part of a proposed greenway.

Zealandia Bridge has been immortalized for all time, not only by persistent ghostly rumors, but also by author Thomas Wolfe who lived in the area and spent time near the bridge. Wolfe incorporated it into his 1929 novel, *Look Homeward, Angel*:

> "They turned from the railing, with recovered wind, and walked through the gap, under Philip Roseberry's great arched bridge... As they

went under the shadow of the bridge Eugene lifted his head and shouted. His voice bounded against the arch like a stone. They passed under and stood on the other side of the gap, looking from the road's edge down into the cove."

When did Zealandia Bridge become Helen's Bridge? No one knows for sure when, or who Helen really is. Some rumors claim that the name comes from Helen Clevenger, who was murdered in the Battery Park Hotel, not far from the bridge. Helen's tormented soul may be walking the bridge for all eternity. But, a more common story attributes the name to a woman who suffered a tragic set of circumstances at Zealandia castle itself.

Local folklore says that, during the 1930s, a woman named Helen lived with her daughter in a small cottage near the Zealandia mansion. One version of the story says that Helen worked at the castle and brought her daughter along one day. Another version says the daughter sneaked off to play at the house on her own. However the girl arrived there, the day took a tragic turn when she was killed in a rampaging fire. Distraught over her daughter's horrible death, Helen took a length of rope to Zealandia Bridge and hung herself.

Other theories suggest that the fire took place in Helen's own home, resulting from a cooking accident in the kitchen. Yet other versions report that Helen was John Evans Brown's mistress, and, after becoming pregnant, she hung herself in anguish. Regardless of who Helen may actually have been, many people traveling on College Street near the bridge report a number of odd occurrences in that area, going back 50 years and through the present day.

As the legend goes, you can conjure the appearance of Helen's spirit by standing under the bridge and repeating three times: either the name "Helen" or the phrase "Helen, come forth!" She may appear as a light or as the apparition of a pale woman in a flowing gown. After the woman appears, she will ask, "Have you seen my daughter?"

Sometimes Helen can appear even without being summoned. One man who never believed in the paranormal before was riding a motorcycle when he saw a woman near the bridge in white, old-fashioned clothes. Remembering the rumors, he turned for a better look, but the woman was gone, despite terrain she could not have traversed quickly.

There are frequent reports of unusual occurrences by many people who have attempted to raise Helen's spirit at the bridge, or have simply visited the location. Cameras that malfunction or stop working entirely are reported often. Photos that are taken commonly show strange mists or figures who were not there when the picture was taken. One photo taken by a group of boys visiting the site did not show the four boys by the bridge, but only blackness with a strange misty haze. Some visitors report that they could hear someone walking across the bridge as they stood below it even though no one was visible there.

Social media and publications are littered with reports that people who drive to Helen's Bridge have trouble starting their car or have other mechanical problems with their vehicle when they try to leave the location. One person reported sitting in their car near the bridge with the key turned off, nonetheless, the radio saw fit to turn on and start playing. Sometimes cell phone batteries are unexpectedly drained and die. Numerous accounts claim that, after being near the bridge, mysterious hand prints appear on the outside of their car. The prints will show on the door or window glass and sometimes cannot be removed.

One author investigating the bridge returned to her car to find the automatic locks malfunctioning. The problem continued for a week until she returned to the bridge and pleaded with Helen to leave the car alone. She was shocked to find that the problem no longer occurred.

Copious research on the subject of Helen has turned up no definitive proof who Helen was, or if she ever truly existed. This has led some to suggest alternate theories to explain the haunting of Zealandia Castle and Helen's Bridge.

One such theory is that the spook reported in these locations is that of Violet Henry, the wife of Sir Henry who died in the New York fire. Perhaps her restless spirit came here to be with her loved ones, haunting the halls of the home she was meant to have, but never visited during her lifetime. Perhaps Violet's actual death in a fire is what sparked the rumors of the Helen's daughter having her life tragically ended in flames. And, if this theory is accurate, it might explain why some owners of Zealandia have encountered an apparition of a woman on the stairs in the home.

One woman who visited the Zealandia office building insisted that she had heard noises that she couldn't explain. "I do think it has something going on there, for sure," she declared. "I have a friend that works there at an office. Sometimes we'd go by to see her and you could hear weird noises going on upstairs where nobody was. I was like, 'What's up there?' 'Nothing.' Well, I could definitely hear stuff. My friend was like, 'Yeah, I've heard some stuff. I just don't think anything about it.'"

Another alternate theory involves a tragedy in the area near the bridge that actually can be confirmed. On May 6, 1906, the Asheville Gazette published an article about a man named James Monery who committed suicide with a shot to his head in the location where the bridge would be built three short years later. Monery was an employee of Phillip S. Henry, then owner of Zealandia. Is Monery responsible for the strange events that take place at the bridge? Or will Helen's true story someday be known? Only time will tell. For now, the brave among us can stand beneath the bridge and call Helen's name. When she appears, steel your nerves and ask her.

ZEALANDIA ESTATE IS PRIVATE PROPERTY. HELEN'S BRIDGE ON COLLEGE STREET IS OWNED BY THE CITY OF ASHEVILLE. IF YOU VISIT, DO NOT GO ONTO THE BRIDGE OR TRESPASS ON ZEALANDIA PROPERTY. USE CAUTION WITH TRAFFIC NEAR THE BRIDGE.

Helen's Bridge and Zealandia References

Carla. "Trivia: Why is there a castle in Asheville, NC called Zealandia?" *Greetings From the Past*. https://www.greetingsfromthepast.com/2017/03/trivia-why-is-there-a-castle-in-asheville-nc-called-zealandia-why-is-there-an-area-in-new-zealand-called-swannanoa/ Web. Posted March 29, 2017. Web. Accessed May 3, 2020.

"Helen's Bridge (Asheville, North Carolina)." *Haunt Hub*. https://haunthub.wordpress.com/ghosts-haunts/helens-bridge-asheville-north-carolina/. Web. Accessed May 3, 2020.

"Helens Bridge: Asheville, NC." *Try To Scare Me*. https://www.trytoscare.me/legend/helens-bridge-asheville-nc-2/ Web. Accessed May 3, 2020.

McDaniel, Polly. "Asheville ghost story: Helen's bridge." *The City of Asheville*. https://www.ashevillenc.gov/news/asheville-ghost-story-helens-bridge/. Posted October 13, 2019. Web. Accessed May 3, 2020.

Powell, Lewis. "Resting high on that mountain--Helen's Bridge, Asheville." *Southern Spirit Guide*. http://www.southernspiritguide.org/resting-high-on-that-mountain-helens-bridge-asheville/. Published December 31, 2015. Web. Accessed May 3, 2020.

Southern Living. (2017, September 11.) *Zealandia Mansion* [Video]. YouTube. https://www.youtube.com/watch?v=71uoGqIX9fY.

Wikipedia contributors. "Zealandia (Asheville, North Carolina)." https://en.wikipedia.org/wiki/Zealandia_(Asheville,_North_Carolina) *Wikipedia, The Free Encyclopedia*. Web. Accessed November 7, 2018.

WLOS News 13. (2020, May 3.) *Special Report: Haunting of Helen's Bridge*. [Video]. YouTube. https://www.youtube.com/watch?v=hL3UHLzSqbo.

Zepke, Terrance. "Best Ghost Tales of North Carolina." Pineapple Press, 2006. Print. Pages 75-77.

OTHER BOOKS BY TRACY L. ADKINS
Now available online and at local booksellers

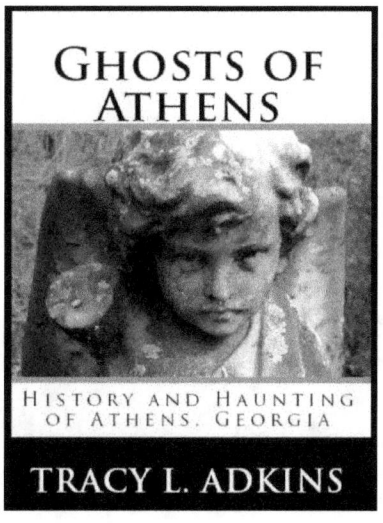

About the Author

Tracy L. Adkins was born in Fort Lauderdale, Florida and has been writing and journaling since she was knee-high to a June bug. She moved to North Georgia at age nine for an idyllic childhood on a 500-acre farm nestled on the Etowah River. She graduated from high school in Blue Ridge, Georgia before beginning studies at Berry College and later graduating from the University of Georgia. She fell in love with Athens, Georgia upon her arrival in 1990 and has remained there since with the exception of a brief stint in Asheville, North Carolina, where she still loves to visit. She eventually spent 17 years writing software instructions, but decidedly prefers to compose prose, poetry, screenplays, and historical books. She spends her days in Athens writing and spoiling her four cats.

Tracy at her desk in 2017
with Grace, a very good boy